Northumberland and The Sinister Side

CRIME AND PUNISHMENT 1837-1914

INTRODUCTION

At the start of Victoria's reign most people lived in small towns and villages, large numbers of felons were transported and public hangings were regularly witnessed by enormous drunken, jeering mobs. By its end most people lived in large towns and cities, a massive prison building project had been implemented and murderers were quietly despatched behind closed doors.

The move to the towns created enormous health and accommodation problems in places like Newcastle, Sunderland, Durham and Gateshead where whole families made do with just one squalid room and often shared the same bed.

Life in these teeming towns was brutish and assault common, disputes being swiftly settled with a few well-directed kicks and punches. A majority of offences were committed under the influence of alcohol and cases of wife-beating, petty larceny and the occasional murder filled courts throughout the old counties of Northumberland and Durham.

Most of the reports of life and crime in the North-East, from Berwick to Darlington, are here published for the first time. Please join us in Northumberland and Durham... the Sinister Side.

First published in 1999
Reprinted in 2001

Wicked Publications
222, Highbury Road,
Bulwell
Nottingham NG6 9FE
England
Telephone/Fax (0115) 975 6828
e-mail: wickedbooks@ukonline.co.uk

ISBN 1 870000 49 8

By the same author:

LONDON...THE SINISTER SIDE

WICKED LONDON

THROUGH THE KEYHOLE

CAPITAL PUNISHMENTS

IN DARKEST LONDON

WHEN THE LIGHTS WENT DOWN

NOTTINGHAM...THE SINISTER SIDE

MANCHESTER...THE SINISTER SIDE

BIRMINGHAM...THE SINISTER SIDE

LANCASHIRE LASSES...THEIR LIVES AND CRIMES

see back pages for details

Typeset and printed in Great Britain by:
Parker & Collinson Ltd.
(incorporating DESA Design & Print)
42 Church Street, Lenton, Nottingham

CONTENTS

'FILTHY BEYOND DESCRIPTION'

1. Shut that door! 24-26, Thames Street, South Shields. This was one of the better privies.

Possibly the most revealing accounts of the sheer brutish facts of existence for most people in the nineteenth century come from court reports. 11-year-old William Hepplewhite's shocking testimony at the inquest into his mother's death – South Shields, Christmas Eve, 1875 – describes a way of life all too typical of the North-East, and indeed of most other industrialised regions at the time.

My father, when he came in, was very nigh drunk. My mother was sitting by the fireside bathing her head with vinegar. My father said "what are you doing?" and my mother replied "I am bathing my head." Nothing more was said by either, and my father struck her with his doubled fist on the right side of the forehead. She got up from her seat and sat down upon a chair near the window. Directly she sat down upon the chair he struck her with his fist in the breast.

My mother then said. "Give over, Jim" and he replied, "You b_____." My father then sat down upon a stool and lighted his pipe, my mother meanwhile continuing to bathe her head. My mother afterwards moved to a chair near to the bedside and took off her gown. My father then got up from the stool and struck her with his fist on the left eye and on the right side, knocking her up against a chest of drawers, and down upon the floor. My mother got up and sat down upon the chair. My father sat down, and said, "Billy, get your clothes off and go to bed." My

mother had previously asked me to bathe her head, and I said to my father, "I cannot go to bed until I bathe my mother's head." He then said, "Go to bed" and after I pulled off his boots and coats I went to bed soon afterwards. My mother came to bed and lay down beside me. Shortly after that my father came in by the foot of the bed and lay down between my mother and myself. There was a fire burning brightly. As soon as my father got covered with bed clothes my mother began to cough, and my father put his back against her and pushed her out of bed saying, "Get out you w___ __". My mother lay on the floor all night. I got up next morning about seven o'clock, lighted the fire, and got the kettle to boil. When I got up my mother was lying in the same place as she had fallen with no covering to keep her warm. My father got up at half-past seven. I made him a cup of tea, and went, at my father's request, to the quay to see about some coal. I returned in about half-an-hour and my father was then gone, my mother was still lying in the same position as before. I said, "Mother, get up", but she did not answer and I covered her with some petticoats. I lifted her partly up, but she was unable to sit up or get up, and never spoke. A woman named Charlotte Robson came in to see what time it was. Mrs Robson saw mother lying, and went away for Mrs Clarke. When they returned I went for Margaret Smith, and afterwards for my sister. When I got back at quarter-past one my mother was laying in bed dead.

A verdict of wilful murder against the father was returned and the case sent to the assizes. Hepplewhite senior was sent down for ten years.

The Hepplewhites, in their rented room, were a social step above the transient poor, most of whom were forced to seek shelter in common lodging houses, with the emphasis very much upon the word 'common.' In South Shields in February, 1853, 1,667 people were accommodated in such establishments, two thirds of whom were male. About half of this total, 793, were of Irish descent, 499 were English and 375 were *Scotch*.

In 1851 a health officer painted a harrowing picture of accommodation in Newcastle:

The Lodging-houses are for the most part situated in very narrow and unhealthy lanes, generally about five and a half feet wide, and in some cases not more than three feet wide. In the worst case there are 12 lodgers in a room, 14 x 12 x 8.3 feet wide, allowing an area to each lodger of only 14 square feet, and cubic space to each of 112 feet. The number of beds being 4. There are in each bed three persons.

Across the river conditions were, if anything, more unsavoury. In 1850 the Superintendent of police in Gateshead, William Schorey, described his visit to lodging houses in the Pipewellgate area:

I have had opportunities of witnessing, in rooms measuring not more than 14 feet square, from 15 to 20 men, women and children lodged, the men and children completely naked, with the exception of a small rug and the women with nothing more than a shift, which, from the length of time and the filthy habits of the wearer, had the appearance of oil cloth more than the undergarment of a female; they were all breathing an atmosphere pestilential in the extreme. Added to this, unrestrained sexual intercourse takes place in the presence of the youth of both sexes, not a screen of any kind intervening.

In jam-packed slums youngsters had their first sex-education lessons overhearing the sighs and sobs and swiftly succeeding snoring, of their too proximate elders and betters, scenes which usually occurred following prolonged bouts of whistle wetting.

More fastidious couples adopted desperate measures as their children grew older. An inhabitant of South Shields recalls one solution to the lack of privacy:

I knew a family, the father and the mother had to gan outside to do their business, d'you know what I mean, with them having so many in the house? Yes, they used to do their courtin' outside, the mother and father. Even when they had as far as seven children they used to go outside and do their courting. I was about 14 then and I was gettin' to understand what was goin' on. The mother used to stand at the telegraph pole on Johnson's Hill and have her love with her husband and then gan yem and gan to bed. Them were serious times and all their business was ootside. You couldn't do nowt with all the family living in one room!

2. *Lower Thames Street in South Shields 1910, ran parallel with the river. Many battered wives suffered in silence and a clip round the ear for wayward kids was the norm.*

STABBED WITH A POKER AT SUNDERLAND

3. In densely populated lodging-houses there was the persistent threat of violence. This illustration is from 1878.

In Sunderland lodging houses were concentrated in the east or old part of the town, and, once again *ill-ventilated and crowded to excess.* Here, affrays and assaults were the norm. In February, 1878, in an establishment run by a man named Burns, a quarrel broke out in the kitchen, where there were plainly too many cooks. In the heat of the argument one male lodger, obviously reluctant to get out of the kitchen, fatally stabbed a woman in the neck with a poker. The story warranted an appropriately gory inclusion in the *Illustrated Police News,* but apparently no other warrant!

Durham was home to some forty lodging houses, all of which were *exceedingly ill-managed, close, crowded, dirty...the place where disease is generated.* And these were the licensed houses – it was possible to sink even lower. On Christmas Eve, 1875, housing inspectors called in on Timothy Fallon's house in Moatside Lane. In just one bedroom two beds served the somnolent needs of Timothy, his wife, two step-daughters and six illegal lodgers. For this violation of licensing laws, Fallon was fined £5 or two months.

Yet more disconcerting than such basic overcrowding, were potential sleeping partners, some of whom made bed bugs and lice seem appealing. Inhabitants of lodging houses were typified as:-

The thief who never yet learned the first lessons of moral principle – the tawdry prostitute who casts around her the contagion of vice and disease – the perambulatory theatrical, who earns a subsistence by low and degrading exhibitions, calculated only to excite the worst passions of our nature – and the swarms of vagrants who wander from place to place in quest of alms, or mechanics in search of work – these are the chief components of Low Lodging-House Society.

Here, huddled together irrespective of age or sex, all sense of decency or propriety is exiled, and vice in its varied, and most degrading forms bears triumphant and unquestioned sway.

4. Shadwell Street, South Shields. Woman's lot was one long round of baby bearing and sometimes burying with, even at the start of the twentieth century, more than one child in ten dying before their first birthday. These women probably worked long hours for very poor money and aged before their time. They had no right to vote or sit on juries. One of their few pleasures was a drop or two of drink to mentally escape their very harsh lives.

5. The corner of Salmon's Lane in Shadwell Street in 1892 (South Shields).

The dwellings were crowded, filthy, and bore every appearance of extreme want, and it was found that many people were existing on the lowest possible scale of nourishment, and clothing was deficient amongst them.

The streets and lanes were equally neglected and filthy, nay disgusting, as every impurity was allowed to remain exposed, and many people were found who had accumulated quantities of manure in their houses.

The provision of privies did not grow in proportion to the rapid increases in population. The number of inhabitants in Gateshead tripled to 25,000 between 1811 and 1851. In 1843, the centre of the Irish community, Pipewellgate, contained just three privies for over 2,000 inhabitants. With its various piggeries and 181 tripe shops, the town must have resembled one large slaughterhouse. Indeed the area boasted thirty-one slaughterhouses, all described as offensive, being *several inches deep in blood, offal and dung*. Ironically the pigs probably kept the death rate from disease down being a reasonably healthy means of waste disposal.

The methods of disposal of human waste changed very slowly in the poorer areas, with ash pits continuing even in the early years of thé twentieth century, as one inhabitant of South Shields recalls:

They were all ash toilets in them days. You just used to go into the toilet and away you done yer business, and put a few ashes in out of yer fireplace, and then covered it up. Then the corporation men used to come and shovel it out and throw lime in.

6. Rising damp was not solely attributable to rain in Pipewellgate. The cholera epidemic of 1853 was followed by the Great Fire a year later which destroyed much of Hillgate but left Pipewellgate virtually unscathed. The area was described by health visitors in the middle of the nineteenth century as 'a vile place' and anybody with any money sought residence elsewhere. The banks were landscaped in 1969-70.

The Health of Towns Commission were positively repulsed by the stench of *men, women, children, dogs, dogs-meat and monkies* – though quite where the apes fit in is unclear, refugees from Hartlepool perhaps? They went on to list the numbers of people in each room they visited. The maximum number of males sharing with one woman was 11, while for females 7 to 4 was the highest ratio – a polygamist's dream? In another room, in one bed of normal dimensions, were a father and mother, a grown-up son and daughter and two young children.

It was not just the inhabitants of lodging houses who dwelt in squalor, however. A health commissioner, Dr Morley, described the conditions endured by the majority of the population of Sunderland in the middle of the nineteenth century:

Poor sanitary conditions were exacerbated by the narrow streets. Back in Pipewellgate for example, over 330 yards long, the street with an average width of scarcely 8ft. accommodated the sanitary needs of 2,000 inhabitants, most of whom relieved themselves where they stood, though not, of course, on their own doorsteps! Despite this, however, rising damp was a fact of life.

The origin of the *unhealthy emanations* in Gateshead's narrow streets was put down to the poor provision of sewers and ashpits:

The inhabitants having no other method of disposing of their refuse excrement, but throw them upon the streets and lanes, where they spread, become decomposed and evolve a most disgusting odour, more particularly when the weather is warm and close.

Although there were local acts against such behaviour these were rarely enforced as, like the famous recipe for cooking hares – first you must catch them.

Darlington had similar problems as an inspector of the sanitary committee pointed out:

Who shall prove, in a yard containing fifty or sixty inhabitants that the matter has come from a slaughterhouse, butcher's shop, hogsty or dunghill; or who prove it against?

The Dark Stairs area in North Shields was home for those who could fall no further. Here they are described, by an overtly critical medical officer in the middle of the nineteenth century:

The Dark Stairs is a miserable place inhabited by persons of the lowest and most degraded condition. A dungheap adjoins the entrance from the wooden bridge-bank and at the back of the houses there is a stagnant ditch filled with animal and vegetable refuse matter. This is never cleaned out, though it is the receptacle for the whole of the offal from the dwellings. The place is in a very wretched state; there is filth in every quarter of the court and squalor and misery in every room. There is a pant in the court, but no privy accommodation. Thirty families reside on the Dark Stairs. The rooms are about 13' high and 12' broad and have an average three families in each.

The first port of call in North Shields for the light-fingered was Sally Joyce's lodging house on Stream Mill Bank. Here dips and house-breakers might fence their booty and spend the proceeds on food, ale and accommodation. Sally did not stint on the fare. When health inspectors called they interrupted the lodgers who were voraciously tucking into a feast of roast beef and eggs washed down with copious amounts of tea and hot whiskey toddy. For a few professional pilferers, crime apparently did pay.

Although the tucker was of a high standard the inspectors found the lodgings *filthy beyond description.* Seeking out stolen property, the officials went through the cupboards and, to their revulsion, stumbled across *a deposit of human filth.* Obviously someone had not been bothered to use the ashpit. As may be imagined *the effluvia from the room was most overpowering.*

GATESHEAD

7. The notorious Pipewellgate in Gateshead. In 1843 there was provision for just three privies for 2,000 inhabitants. An area with a very dark history.

8. *Shoes and boots for sale on the quayside in Newcastle. Footwear was one of the prime targets for shoplifters with hundreds of cases coming before the courts every year. When times were hard they may have been pledged at the pawnbrokers. Even in the first years of the twentieth century it was not uncommon to see young boys and girls wandering the cities in bare feet.*

9. Scene from Hartlepool. A very early photograph (1865) showing a man smoking a long clay pipe in Southgate. An indication as to the product available in a shop, perhaps for the benefit of those who could not read, can be seen on top of the building.

In Gateshead, Mary Murphy's Union Street establishment was a mecca for the thieving classes. The landlady came with excellent references, her husband having been transported for highway robbery. When Mary's house posted its No Vacancies sign, George Thew's place in Leonard Court took up the slack. George would always squeeze in a few more paupers, pimps and pickpockets for a few pennies more. In Union Street you paid your money but you had no choice where sleeping partners were concerned.

As always there was no segregation by age and sex in lodging houses, guilt and innocence were sandwiched together. In 1850, the chief police officer in Gateshead claimed that these establishments acted as both nursery and finishing school for the criminal classes.

Not only are such places the hot-beds of disease in its most loathsome forms, but they are sources from which crime, in its deepest dye, may be traced; some of the most daring offences on criminal record having, from time to time been connected with their filthy atmosphere...It is here that the young vagrant comes into contact with the old and experienced thief, and where are discussed the plans and ramifications of the day. Reared up in idleness, and without those lessons of morality which might otherwise be imparted to him, the younger vagrant looks to the older and more daring for instruction in imposture and crime...and further, in connexion with houses of this description, it not unfrequently happens that the keeper is a receiver of stolen property, and acts in the capacity of a fence...

With general health dependent on a steady supply of fresh water, an impossible dream in newly industrialised towns, it is no surprise that disease affected nearly every home. In 1849 in Stockton a health Inspector noted:

A great number of the people derive their supply of water from the public pumps, but the quality is bad, containing a good deal of organic matter, encrusts the tea-kettles, and is entirely unfit for washing.

And it didn't come cheap either:

The poorer classes travel upon an average a distance of 100 yards for their supply of water, or subject themselves to the charge made by the water-carriers of one halfpence for about three gallons. In some instances the charge is 10s. per annum for beverage water only.

Three years previously, in 1846, the mortality rate almost doubled in one year in the large towns of the North-East. The number of people dying in September, 1846, is compared with the previous year:

	SEPTEMBER 1845	SEPTEMBER 1846
NEWCASTLE	423	857
GATESHEAD	165	473
TYNEMOUTH	292	503
SUNDERLAND	292	475

The summer of 1846 was very warm and it was thought that the increased mortality in towns was due to a combination of this factor and *crowded lodgings – dirty dwellings – personal uncleanliness – the concentration of unhealthy emanations from narrow streets without fresh air, water or sewers.* The infant mortality rate was also proportionately higher with an increase in the main child killer diseases of measles, whooping cough, scarlatina (scarlet fever), pneumonia and diarrhoea.

One of the least attractive towns in the North-East was Portrack, near Stockton. Here in the 1870s there was more than enough work, but accommodation was short in all senses of the word. Add to this potentially volatile mixture two large groups of ethnic workers, the Irish and Welsh, who could barely stand the sight of each other, and twelve public-houses and total anarchy was virtually guaranteed, particularly on Saturday nights when Paddys and Taffys communicated by hurling bricks and abuse at each other.

Violence was not solely directed on nationalistic lines as a writer calling himself 'the Stockton Critic' was quick to point out:

In the best times, Portrackians could drink two-three times a week, earn good wages, wear big, heavy boots, kick and thrash their wives in comfort, without much interference from a policeman. Cock fighting, pigeon flying, drinking and dog worrying formed their sovereign delight.

Conditions were not a great deal better in the pit villages where, in the first half of the nineteenth century, one up and one down houses, made of rubble stone, were hastily erected to house colliers and their families. Like the prefabs built one hundred years later, many continued to survive well past their builders' expectations. In 1907 John Wilson summarised the views of most pitmen:

The old-time houses are a standing witness of the opinion those who built them had of the workmen.

10. A woman, a child and shared out-houses in Dovecot Yard, Hartlepool.

11. St. John's Chapel c1914.

Access to the first floor communal bedroom was via a step ladder to what amounted to an attic space above. With many such rooms not fitted with trapdoors, sleepwalkers were in particular danger.

The only way a little privacy was possible – either in sickness or in health! – was by dividing rooms with movable screens, a furnishing also used to protect from draughts. The quaintly termed earth closets were shared by two houses and excreta in the 'netty' was, as ever, covered with ashes.

Nearly every house had a spittoon, often the recipient of chewing tobacco, a habit adopted by miners officially barred from smoking in the pits. Some developed a taste for the weed and would often eat their *bait* (food) *with the chew in their cheek.* With many miners coming from an agricultural background, the occasional keeping of animals supplemented the family diet. Piggeries and privies were a regular feature of most streets until swine fever and local bylaws put pay to the porkers.

The pace of change was slow, and insanitary slave-like working conditions persisted well into the twentieth century. Mary Dixon worked in Stockton as a sanitary inspector. Her job, at the turn of the century, was to check workplaces to ensure that safety regulations were being properly observed. In this capacity the Vicar's daughter came across *poverty, wickedness, hopelessness and ineffectualness.* Her reports included stories of women standing for long hours in soaking wet mud, washing bottles or other people's clothes in backyards; young girls with pale skins and unwashed hands employed in small rooms making sweets; seam-mistresses crammed into unventilated backrooms and derelict warehouses where women would sort through rag-and-bone collections, separating cotton goods, for paper factories and sacks of bones for the glue factory near the bridge.

Sometimes shoddy, squalid living conditions were attributed to the slovenliness of the tenants who rented properties. In the early years of the twentieth century, the burgeoning N.S.P.C.C. were regular visitors to homes where the well-being of children was held to be at risk. In Blyth on All Fools Day 1905, Edward Stephenson and his wife Emily appeared in court charged with neglecting their child *in a manner so as to cause it grievous bodily harm*. The inspector told the court that the house was in a filthy condition; the closet doors had been chopped up for firewood and there was no furniture save a table, chair and some sacking.

Edward was described as *an idle, lazy, worthless being* who had worked for just one day in the previous three months. The three shillings he had earned had been spent on drink. He'd had a job paying twenty-five shillings a week but lost it due to a reluctance to get out of bed much before noon. He much preferred to live off his wife's money: Emily Stephenson was a street-walker. Every night she would leave home at 6 pm, returning five hours later with a different customer. The family home was used for *an improper purpose* with several *loose women* making use of the filthy facilities.

With both husband and wife inebriated when in funds, the poor child, whose gender was never mentioned, was seriously neglected, kept in stinking clothes for days on end, and very rarely changed. There was evidence of vermin bites and two serious burns on the child, whose father had been heard threatening to throw the screaming infant *to the back of the fire*.

Sentenced to three month's each with hard labour, the Stephensons probably considered themselves hard done by, their approach to life being no different to countless others in the same circumstances.

12. Mrs Hodgson with her kippers at Mrs Stevensons, Seaton Carew, 1885-90.

'BASTARD STOLE MY HORSE'

13. Mary Christie had a long list of convictions, mostly for stealing from the person. Of the prisoners in the 1873 Newcastle mug shot book, 184 are male and 82 female. The most common offenders names were William, John, Richard and James and Mary, Mary Ann and Elizabeth.

A typical day's proceedings from Seaham Harbour Petty Sessions on March 3rd 1865 makes for interesting reading into the nature of the crimes of the times:

John Simpson of Australia Row was fined 2/6d for assaulting Mary Ann Davis with whom he had quarrelled about the division of some coals.

John Simon was charged with using threatening language towards John B Irwin, a rent collector. The complainant said he called at one Thomas Burkas's for the property tax, and seeing the defendant's wife there, he advised her to pay her water rate account to avoid a distraint. The defendant then rushed out of a back room and would have committed an assault if he had not been held back by some women. The bench bound John Simon over in his own recognizances to keep the peace.

Joseph Richardson, a one-legged man, was charged with indecently assaulting Miriam Waller, a half-witted deaf girl, but as there was not sufficient evidence to make a whole case, the matter was dropped.

William Young was fined 1 shilling and costs for assaulting Hannah Clerk at East Murton.

Robert Mullen, who got very drunk and insisted upon visiting the Noah's Ark beerhouse after hours, assaulted the landlord, who would not let him in. He was fined 10 shillings and costs.

John Deacon, Thomas Paxton and Jacob Milburn were fined 1d damage and costs for trespassing on land belonging to Mr George Welsh.

Edward Wilson was charged with a severe assault upon a widowed relative, Margaret Fairley. The assault arose out of a quarrel about family affairs and the evidence was very conflicting, but as the Bench thought the weight of it was in support of the complaint, they inflicted a fine of twenty shillings and costs.

John Evans was fined 1s and costs for assaulting Hugh Simon, a boy. Defendant pleaded that the youth made use of indecent language towards his wife, and therefore he thought he was justified in thrashing him. Who could possibly object?

14. Mary Sherrin followed the all too well-trodden downhill path of female convicts. Three convictions for drunkenness, for which she spent 28 days inside, were followed by charges of vagrancy and prostitution. She then found a new hobby - assaulting policemen - which led to a further two months' drying out. Convictions for being a rogue and vagabond and for 'larceny from the person' followed. We see her here, in 1873, about to serve three months, with almost certainly many more years of bird-lime to come.

15. 51-year-old William Harrison, sentenced to one year for obtaining money under false pretences. Most male offenders listed their profession as labourer whilst female offenders were prostitutes, charwomen and servants, in that order.

In 1849 Morpeth Michael Walton was found guilty of stealing two tame turkeys and ten tame hens and sentenced to 14 years' transportation. In the same court 34-year-old William Lee was convicted of stealing a cotton gown which the owner had spread over a hedge to dry. He was sentenced to be privately whipped and to serve two months imprisonment, with one week of each month to be served in solitary. Another young lad sentenced to transportation was a defiant 16-year-old burglar, Henry James Richards, who annoyed the bench in 1846 by addressing the pronouncing judge as follows:

Speak up, I cannot hear what you say.

The judge repeated: *The sentence of the court is that you be transported for ten years.*

Henry was determined to have the last word: *Thank you, that will do.* Henry obviously interpreted the sentence as a free cruise to the land of opportunity.

Not all sentences were so harsh. That same year in Newcastle James Wilson, who found the case a drag, was fined 2/6d for being dressed in women's clothes and creating a disturbance in Sandgate. Elizabeth Carter *a girl of the town* was charged by James Renshaw with robbing him of tuppence ha'penny. James testified that he felt her hand in his pocket. And he complained?! When examined at the police station the money was found to be in the accused's possession but the magistrates considered the matter of small importance and had it discharged.

16. John Park a 19-year-old soldier of the 14th Brigade R.A. who would have liked to have been on the fiddle. He was sentenced to one month with hard labour for stealing a violin.

Besides the national code, citizens of the North-East had their own various bye-laws which addressed specific problems of the times. In 1849, amongst other prohibitions, the inhabitants of Morpeth were not allowed to:-

1. Shake, beat or dust any carpet, mat or furniture in any of the streets after 9 am.

2. Leave out 'night-soil', offal, putrid meat or fish, entrails of fish, carrion, dead animals, blood, dung, manure, bones, refuse of vegetables, stagnant water or any other offensive matter (fine not exceeding £5).

3. Indecently and wilfully expose their person (fine not more than £5, not less than £2).

4. Exhibit, show, sell or distribute any obscene or indecent print, drawing, painting, representation, ballad, pamphlet or book (fine not exceeding £5).

Locals were also expected to *cleanse, amend and repair* footpaths adjoining their tenements and also to go to the assistance of the police or face a fine of up to £5.

17. Ella Brown, a 25-year-old prostitute with eleven previous convictions. She was sent down for four months for obtaining money under false pretences. Ella looks a hard no-nonsense character, well capable of looking after herself inside and out!

Inevitably the majority of the prison population spent only a few days or weeks inside. A large proportion of offenders were paupers who had no money to pay fines. They often faced prison as the result of refusing to perform designated tasks in the workhouses. The 1874 case of a tramp in Hartlepool featured in court reports under the headline *Teaching The Lazy How To Work*. John Wilson, a strong, healthy looking fellow, was charged with refusing to work in a Hartlepool workhouse. After having been provided food and lodgings Wilson was presented the following morning with 3cwt of stones. He was ordered to break them down, a chore not out of place within the prison regime. After smashing two stones, Wilson, quite reasonably, threw down the hammer and refused to continue. When asked in court if he had anything he swiftly replied, *It's quite true. I've nothing to say.* He was sentenced to two weeks' hard labour and doubtless a few altercations with the turnkeys.

Some characters were in and out of the cells so often they acquired nicknames. One such character was the 'Hasswell Gaol Bird' – Robert Suggat who refused to leave public houses and would never pay fines. He may well have been tempted to change the habits of a lifetime had he been billeted next to Ann Cornwell. Charged in 1875 with being disorderly in Framwellgate, Annie the drunkard entertained her fellow detainees and *amused herself with singing, nearly all night, in a very loud tone.* The melodious cage bird was sent to perform at Durham for one month.

Following sentencing many offenders were dragged away swearing vengeance on the judge. Nineteen-year-old Isabella Reilly, however, a girl with a long list of convictions, appeared to bear no ill-will. After being sentenced to seven years for stealing a purse containing £10.15s. she simply stated: *'I hope I'll come back a better woman.'*

Relatively minor offences were usually harshly punished by today's standards and the main culprits were young lads. Gambling was very much frowned upon and anyone found *racing dogs on the highway* was commonly fined 20s. Young people were regularly prosecuted for playing pitch and toss, or fined for such offences as snowballing and sliding on the footpath.

18. Sabina Forbes aka Purvis Clark and Elizabeth Crudace. The longer the form the higher the sentence so many prisoners used aliases. If her attire is anything to go by, 32-year-old Sabina had hit rock bottom and may have welcomed a stay inside following convictions for prostitution, assault and being a rogue and vagabond.

19. *John Gordon Junior. Whipping and reform school were no deterrent for those determined to pursue a life of crime.*

The police certainly had it in for Peter McKenna of Monkwearmouth in 1873. He was accused of creating a disturbance by whistling, dancing and singing, with others, in John Street. P.C. Short testified that he heard Peter shout *Cheese my lads,* after which his merrymaking accomplices fled. When asked the meaning of 'cheese' the policeman smiled and replied *It is a slang phrase meaning; Beware the police are at hand.* Because of his long string of convictions Peter was fined a very harsh 40 shillings.

It's unlikely that P.C. Golightly of Hartlepool lived up to his name in 1900 when interviewing two likely lads. In the days long before taped interviews the constable composed the alleged confessions of 11-year-old Oswald Smith and 9-year-old Bertie Pickering. According to Golightly's notes the boys owned up to stealing underwear in the following unambiguous manner:

PICKERING: *Yes, I took the drawers.*

SMITH: *Yes, I was with Pickering when he took the drawers, and I attempted to pledge them at Thompson's pawnshop in Park road.*

In Hartlepool that same year a young man, Henry Connolly, was charged with larceny. Upon arriving at his shop at 20, Tennant Street a grocer, George Rutter, found that his front window had been smashed and a large loaf of bread grabbed. The thief had the temerity to be found consuming the evidence on the spot. Connolly was either a very cool customer or just plain daft. His comments in court certainly favour the latter:

CONNOLLY: *Didn't I sit down and eat it? You wouldn't have copped me if I had run off.*

In custody the thief argued that he ought to get leave to eat the bread seeing that it was in his possession. Asked where he would like to be tried he replied:

CONNOLLY: *I'll be tried at Durham, I'll get som'at to eat there.*

CLERK OF THE COURT: If you are tried here you will probably get that.

CONNOLLY: *Well you can try me here.*

CLERK: *Are you guilty or not guilty?*

CONNOLLY: *I wouldn't mind eating the loaf. I want to eat the loaf that's all... You know they reckon I'm daft, but I'm not.*

MR ROBINSON MURRAY: *You are sentenced to 21 days' hard labour.*

CONNOLLY: *Thanks.*

Quite what happened to the loaf is unclear, but certainly our young hero wouldn't go short of his preferred nourishment, together with a little liquid refreshment, given the then prison regime.

20. *Henry Stephenson came before the court at the age of 12. Would his sentence of two months imprisonment, with solitary confinement at the beginning and end of his time, deter him from a life of crime?*

21. *The crime is unimportant. Is this a true portrayal of Victorian life? Mary Patterson (right) is dressed in the most basic of fashions. She has the wrists and hands of a man, she appears to be losing her hair and according to police records is just 25-years-old. A truly haunting photograph from 1873.*

Children, carefully tutored by their parents, would often give evidence to corroborate a false alibi. One little girl told the court that her father had not been drinking between 1 and 6 pm as he had been shaving all afternoon. The magistrate could not let this pass, telling the court that it couldn't take that long unless he had a blunt razor. When released on bail, the father hinted he might use the cut-throat for another job, telling the magistrate: *I will return if I am living.*

Youngsters were often encouraged into lives of crime by parents who acted as receivers. William Baynes and his mother Grace appeared before the West Hartlepool magistrates: the boy for stealing five stones of coals and his mother for receiving and secreting same. William pleaded guilty and was sentenced to six strokes with the birch rod. Grace sought the sympathy of the court attributing her untypical behaviour to an accident:

I am very sorry, your worships, but I had a very heavy fall from a ladder when cleaning windows a short time since.

The novelty of the defence and her previous good character resulted in her just paying costs.

22. Pratt's Passage, The Croft, Hartlepool. In a civil case a woman was taken to court for stringing her line across a main road. The complainant argued that in the dark he might get caught and fall from his horse.

23. Mary Kinnigan, (13) one of four girls charged with stealing iron in Newcastle, 1873. They were probably caught collecting scrap metal and selling it on for a pittance.

24. Mary Docherty, (14). The girls ages ranged from 11-14, though their shawls and hairstyles were probably very similar to those of their grandmothers.

25. Red-headed Ellen Woodman (11) had trouble seeing her accusers, standing in the dock at just 4' 3".

26. Rosanna Watson, (14) the fourth member of the gang of iron-stealers. Despite extensive research no details of the crime seem to have appeared in the local press. For any amateur sleuths the girls were convicted on May 2nd. 1873 and sentenced to seven days'.

23

24

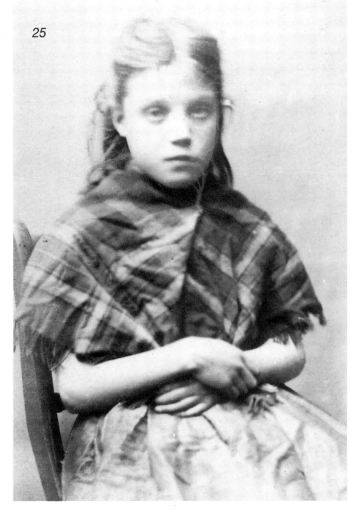

25

26

Another case of taking coals, this time from Newcastle, came before the police court in December, 1869. 18-year-old Elizabeth Donelly and Ann Cain (11) had been told by nearby hoaxers that some coals recently landed at New Quay were charity coals for the use of the poor. In next to no time the greater part of fifteen tons had been spirited away in all manner of receptacles. A large army of women wrapped in shawls, aided by ragged-trousered children, made several trips between the port and home. Elizabeth and Ann, who believed they were doing nothing wrong, were caught carrying coals away but a sympathetic court dismissed the charge. Some of the coal that hadn't already gone up in smoke was later returned, via their children, by poor, but honest, local mothers.

One of the strangest cases heard in Sunderland, 1873, was brought against seven girls, including Fanny and Jane Curry. They were charged with blocking the footpath in Fawcett Street by carrying baskets of rhubarb on their heads. Apparently this unsocial act forced other pedestrians into the gutter. Common sense prevailed, the girls were let off as the case crumbled. Another story from Sunderland, ten years later, saw 15-year-old George Paulin in the dock. He stood accused of shouting in the street and hitting passersby with an animal bladder. A policeman seized the *offending weapon* and, after cutting it up, marched the lad home to obtain his name. Once again, however, the bench deflated the police by dismissing their overblown case.

Strange cases were not confined to the towns. In what seems like an early example of direct action several youths took on the might of a local farmer and were subsequently charged with wilfully damaging turnips. In 1873, Adam Nesbit stood in the dock for working a plough in a field at Brandon without having any person on the road with a flag. In the same court a youth was fined 2/6d for throwing orange-peel onto the path. Mary Ann Adamson, a washerwoman, was charged with hanging out clothes in Newbottle – she'd strung her line across a public highway! The fine for being drunk in charge of a mule and cart was 20/- whilst leaping from a moving railway train cost James Graham, aka Brigham Young (!), £2. Three other characters appearing before the courts for minor offences, Agnes Donking, Jabez Balls and Lancelot Horn, ought perhaps to have considered using alternative names, or maybe they were?

Notions of the print media being responsible for a decline in moral standards are far from new. In April 1879 two Sunderland lads, George Cleminson (17) and William Clark (15), appeared in court charged with stealing two hens. Having boiled and eaten one fowl in some derelict buildings, they were waiting for the second to cook when they were spotted and arrested. Both lads had in their possession novels of the 'penny dreadful' variety namely *Jack Sheppard; The Backwoodsman* and *Chief of Spies*. The head constable told the court that they had evidently *got their head turned by reading such trash.* The elder lad was sentenced to two months' bird while the younger got one.

Victorian tales of boys being sent up chimneys were not fiction. In 1872 eight-year-old Christopher Drummond was ordered to clean the flues, just 12″ in diameter, in a Washington house. The stripling failed to return after his third entry and an even younger, smaller boy was sent in to fetch him. Christopher was found to have suffocated to death. His master Thomas Clark, chimney-sweep, was found guilty of manslaughter and sent down for six months.

Civil cases frequently came before the courts. The most common of such cases was the all too prevalent wife-beating and next came disputes between neighbours. Magistrates had to sit through long, rambling, often incomprehensible, accounts of lengthy disputes as first one neighbour, then the other, slagged each other off. In July, 1875, Margaret Simpson was brought to court by Mary Stephenson on a charge of assault. Mary complained that she had just finished cleaning her doorstep when Margaret came out and brushed the dirt from her step onto hers. When admonished in prime pit language, Margaret ripped off Mary's spectacles, trampled them underfoot and struck her in the face. The long-running Evenwood dispute had apparently started when Mary had thrown tea leaves and dirt onto Margaret's step. The chairman of the court told the protagonists that it was the greatest nonsense he had ever listened to and, in an evenhanded gesture, ordered the women to settle the costs between them.

One of the biggest attractions in the mid-Victorian era, particularly popular with the female population, were the illegal prize fights held in Blyth Links. Here crowds of up to three and four hundred gathered to witness the spectacle of grown men beating each other to a pulp. A main attraction of 1846 was the bout between William Cleghorn of Newcastle and Michael Riley from Gateshead.

The men fought over forty-nine rounds, for two and three-quarter hours, before the man from north of the river was finally declared the winner. The pair shook hands, whereupon Cleghorn, throwing up his hat and pocketing his £10 prize money, blithely ran to a nearby carriage, clearly bent on spending his winnings at once, probably in his favourite inn. His defeated opponent repaired to the Ridley Arms, where he died the next day.

Cleghorn, much to his surprise and annoyance, was subsequently tried for manslaughter. In court, some five months later, he argued that his opponent had been taller, stronger and heavier than himself and that he felt very much hard done by when sentenced to six month's imprisonment.

Few Victorians lived to celebrate their ninetieth birthday and fewer still appeared before the beak at such an advanced age. A wily old conman, William McLeod, aged 91 proved the exception to the rule. In Willington 1873, he stood accused of obtaining money from William Forster, pitman, under false pretences. In a con the nonagenarian must have used countless times, McLeod presented himself to Mrs Forster, confiding to her that he had been left a vast Australian fortune of around £11,000. He claimed that he wanted to find a kind, respectable family with whom he could pass the rest of his days, in return for which he would make them his beneficiaries. Once the Forsters had swallowed the bait, the old scoundrel said that he needed 17/6d in legal fees to facilitate the inheritance. The money trousered,

27. Washerwoman at work. There appears to be a complaint about the brightness of the wash.

McLeod hit the road in pursuit of more soft touches. Finally apprehended in Shotley Bridge, MacLeod very nearly slipped through the net. Because of his age the judge was minded to acquit but once briefed on the number of MacLeod's previous cons, his worship was forced to detain the artful lodger.

Although crime was rife throughout the North-East there were occasional lulls in activity. Indeed, at Hartlepool petty sessions, February 1889, the magistrates were informed that the charge sheet was clear, there were no cases to be dealt with. As this had

happened only on two previous occasions during the last fifty years the event was cause for celebration. This took the somewhat ironical form of the presentation of a pair of size eight-and-a-half white kid gloves to the magistrate, Alderman Horsley. In his acceptance speech the alderman graciously and roundly praised the police and law-abiding citizens of the borough.

COURT REPORTING

A typical day's headlines from the *Newcastle Daily Journal*, January 3rd. 1873 included:

SUDDEN DEATHS AT SOUTH SHIELDS
SMUGGLERS AT SUNDERLAND
FALL DOWN A FLIGHT OF STAIRS IN HEXHAM
BRUTAL ASSAULT ON A WIFE IN NORTH SHIELDS
ASSAULTING A CONSTABLE AT SUNDERLAND

None, however, could match this headline from an 1866 copy of the *Shields Daily News* : **BASTARD STOLE MY HORSE.** In a burst of creative enterprise, more than a century ahead of its time, the report referred to the case of John Bastard, a notorious horse-thief, up to his old tricks again.

Early reports, before the introduction of photography, contained details as to the appearance and demeanour of prisoners in the dock. Predictably reporters' descriptions of the accused would fail most of today's political correctness tests. Defendants were variously described as: *a dissipated-looking woman, a distressed-looking woman, a blackguard-looking fellow, two bad-looking characters, apparently a Quadroon or Mulatto, a rough-looking Irishman with closely-cropped hair, a voluble old lady and a poor, miserable old woman.*

28   JAMES WELCH, AGED 23.

On rare occasions line drawings were also in evidence. Two such illustrated murder cases were reported in the *Newcastle Advertiser* in March, 1847. Both homicides were the result of fights between young men. 23-year-old James Welch was sentenced to hang for the murder of Thomas Proud near Hexham. Lengthy witness statements were followed by a description of the prisoner :

Welch is considerably under the middle stature, and by no means stout. On entering the dock, he appeared much dejected, and though he stood during the trial, repeatedly shed tears. When the jury retired, he sat down at the end of the dock, and remained in a bending posture, supporting his head with his hand, during nearly the whole of their absence. His agitation increased when the jury returned , and on the delivery of their verdict, he appeared about to fall. Supported by one of the turnkeys, he stood during the learned judge's impressive address, weeping, however freely; and at the close was led away.

29   GEORGE MATTHEWS, AGED 20.   JOHN HUGHES, AGED 25.

A second trial saw 20-year-old George Matthews and John Hughes (25) charged with the wilful murder of Daniel Hives at Longbenton. The younger man was found guilty and sentenced to hang. Hughes was acquitted. Let's join the court reporter, once again at the conclusion of the trial:

On entering the dock in the morning both the prisoners manifested complete composure and pleaded not guilty in a firm voice. Hughes retained his coolness throughout the trial. As it proceeded, Matthews presented a more anxious look, and when the verdict was pronounced, wrung his hands and looked imploringly towards the judge, at the same time saying, "Oh, my Lord." During his lordship's address, the unhappy man repeatedly ejaculated, "My lord, I never did it willingly."

Matthews has a heavy but by no means forbidding countenance. Hughes appears personally to be one of the better class of navigators.

A MURDEROUS DWARF AT DURHAM

30. The vertically-challenged William Smith: sent down for six months following a vicious attack on his wife.

A clerk arraigned for the murder of his wife in 1874 was described as:

rather a good-looking man of middle height with heavy military moustache and short, thick sandy-coloured beard.

In this case, however, the felon's good looks were no advantage, he was convicted and sentenced to hang.

◆

DURHAM CITY POLICE.

THE RESULT OF BEING "ANKLED IN" WITH A DRINKING PARTY.—Mary Ann Smith, a married woman, from Jarrow, was charged with having been drunk in the Market-place. The defendant was found, at one o'clock on Saturday morning drunk in the Market-place, and having no place to go to was provided with lodgings in the police station. The defendant said she got "ankled in" with a party, got too much drink, and having no bed to go to, had taken up her quarters under the Monument.—Discharged on promising to leave the town.

RETURNING TO THE PLACE FROM WHENCE SHE CAME:—Jane Ann Martin was charged with having been drunk in the Market-place on Saturday night. The defendant had been committed to the county prison from Hartlepool, and had only been discharged that morning.—Mr H. J. Marshall : The persons who supply the drink to such like are even more culpable than these poor creatures.—Mr Peele : It is a legitimate business, Mr Marshall.—Mr Marshall : But they ought not to go on filling them drink until they make them drunk. It is those who supply the drink to such cattle as these who do all the mischief.—The defendant was sent to prison for seven days, and cautioned not to remain in the town when again liberated.

HIS FIRST OFFENCE.—John Shaw, of Gilesgate, a young man, was charged with having been drunk in Gilesgate. The defendant, who had been guilty of no disorder, earnestly implored forgiveness, as it was the first time he had ever been before a magistrate. He was admonished and discharged.

"NASTY ANSWERS."—Sarah Green was charged with having been drunk and disorderly in Framwellgate, on Saturday night. The defendant said she had been insulted by some blackguards, and was giving them "nasty answers."—Committed to prison for one month.

31. Typical report from the Durham Chronicle, 1875.

Frequently words and phrases used in old court reports have completely different meanings today. Susan Ryan, a young married woman took the last horse and cart from Howden to Jarrow on Boxing Day 1902. When she would not pay her fare the police were called, and, after refusing to divulge her name and address, she was taken to the police station, ironically the route went right past her home. One might feel sorry for the police officer for the ear-bashing at the time but in today's language he had quite an eventful journey as *'She tongued him all the way; it was awful. It was just like as if her tongue was driven by electric.'*

The *Illustrated Police News* had the largest circulation of any periodical of its time, perhaps due to the deliberately sensationalised manner in which cases, both from home and abroad, were presented. Replete with Illustrations of giant sea monsters, abductions by gorilla, cannibalism, suicide and grisly hatchet jobs, most of which found their ways to the front covers, the attraction of the *IPN* is all too obvious.

One article (pictured), from the June 18th 1881 edition, was probably only featured because of the physical appearance of the prime suspect. Vertically challenged and in need of counselling in order to fully understand his aggressive tendencies, the perpetrator was simply dismissed by the *IPN* as *a murderous dwarf*. William Smith had been spotted by members of the Durham Rowing Club thrashing at his wife with a stick in an attempt to force her into the river. The young athletes intervened and confiscated the weapon, whereupon an even more enraged Smith drew a secreted cobbler's knife and rushed at his wife, swearing he would take her life. Again disarmed, he was handed over to the police and eventually caged for six months.

CRUELTY TO A LUNATIC AT SUNDERLAND

32. The mentally ill were often simply locked away in an upstairs attic. In 1870 the 'Illustrated Police News' published a drawing and report about a woman named Mary whom they alleged was chained naked and ill-treated by her carer, a Mrs Armstrong. There were two sides to the story, however and the paper was forced to report the truth a few weeks later.

The *IPN* did not let facts get in the way of a good story. In September, 1870, the paper ran a report concerning cruelty to a 'lunatic' in Sunderland. Following a tip off, a police officer called in on Mrs Armstrong's house at 96, Mainsforth Terrace, New Hendon. Constable Peacock had called to investigate rumours that a woman was being kept in chains in an upstairs bedroom.

Mrs Armstrong confirmed there was a woman living on the first floor but refused permission for the policeman to visit her. She asked the officer to come back at 10 am when he would be introduced to the woman in question. Peacock refused to leave the house and insisted the lodger be produced within the hour.

Mrs Armstrong eventually came downstairs clutching the arm of a thinly-clad woman of haggard appearance who, on being questioned, claimed she had been confined and chained to her bed. Contact with fresh air quickly made her giddy and, as she sat to rest, Peacock insisted on inspecting her room. He probably wished he hadn't.

The stench was so strong that the officer gagged and had to beat an immediate retreat. Taking deep breaths, he forced himself to do his duty and re-entered the malodorous chamber. The sole contents comprised of a bedstead and a square broken box which served as a dinner table. The window was nailed shut and there were ropes lying about the floor. The woman, Mary, who said she had been confined there nine years, later told police she had been beaten and chained up in a state of nudity and otherwise badly used. She was taken away to the Union.

On the face of it this was an horrendous case of cruelty, but a different scenario was depicted in court. Mrs Armstrong's defence argued that the police failed to find any chains and that Mary had been examined by a surgeon who found no evidence of ill-usage. In fact, physically, she was in a good state of health. She was, however, mentally unstable and, like the *IPN*, had trouble telling fact from fiction. Mrs Armstrong had been given money by Mary's relations to look after her, and regularly took her out on walks. It was impossible for Mary to have been locked up in the room for nine years as the house was only three years old.

Although many of the reported facts were erroneous Mrs Armstrong had, like thousands of others in a similar position, broken the law. She was charged with receiving into her house and taking charge of a lunatic, Mary Ann Hobson, for profit without having an order and medical certificate. Furthermore, her house was not licensed for the reception of lunatics and was not a registered hospital. Also charged with shaming and ill-using the said lunatic, Mrs Armstrong was sent down for three months. Hobson's choice now lay between the workhouse and another 'carer'.

BEVVIED, BOISTEROUS AND BELLIGERENT

33. Unnamed Newcastle pub c1910. A brief escape from the drudgery of home life.

Not surprisingly the majority of cases which came before the court were alcohol-related. On a typical morning in Newcastle – July 30th 1883 – fifty-four prisoners were tried. Of these, forty-four were charged with having been drunk and disorderly; six with fighting; one with having, whilst drunk, assaulted a railway officer; one with having attempted to rescue a prisoner from custody; one with having, whilst drunk, assaulted a police officer. There was a single case of larceny. The only sober offender was the thief. Many of the arresting officers would also have partaken of a bevvy or two: drinking on duty was the most common punishable police offence.

Arrests in South Shields in 1900 show the significant relationship between crime and the consumption of alcohol:

ARRESTS IN SOUTH SHIELDS IN 1900			
CRIME	MALE	FEMALE	TOTAL
Drunkenness	804	316	1,120
Larceny	198	45	243
Assault on P.C.	65	8	73
Prostitution	-	71	71
Common assault	56	7	63
Bye-laws	24	13	37
Cruelty to children	9	11	20
Railway crime	6	1	7

Drinking and assaulting police-officers were two of the favoured pastimes of pitmen. Miners would probably argue that the converse was also true. George Tarry and friend chose St. Valentine's Day, 1873, to undertake a drinking spree. On the Sunday afternoon the two pitmen engaged a cab in Durham and were driven to drink in Sunderland. En route they wouldn't miss a pub, refreshing themselves at each and every alehouse they passed. By the completion of their journey they were well and truly oiled or, as the local newspaper quaintly put it, *fairly overcome by their many potations.* Passing through Sunderland High Street, the cab halted at the Ship Inn. Though tired and emotional the two men considered themselves as bona fide travellers. The landlord of their last halt, however, disagreed and refused them entry. PC 82, who had the misfortune to be passing by at the critical time, went to the assistance of Tarry, who had collapsed in the gutter.

Once upright, the pitman thanked him by tearing the front buttons off the policeman's uniform and swinging wildly at his perceived enemy. His accomplice, whom Tarry refused to grass up in court, had the presence of mind to leg it, otherwise he too would have endured a month's sobriety in one of Her Majesty's hotels.

There were literally thousands of cases of pitmen, and sometimes their wives, coming before the courts charged with assault following drinking binges. In July, 1875, William Armstrong, a miner, was summoned on a charge of assaulting Margaret Short. Following a swilling session he went to her home and bluntly asked if she

34. *A group of Northumberland miners. Pitmen were no strangers to the courts and were regularly fined for drunken affrays.*

needed a man? Rejected, the smooth talker struck her face three times with his clenched fist. Questioned as to why he had assaulted Ms Short, Armstrong simply replied that *he had a mind to*. Fined £1 for the assault, the pitman was immediately paraded in the dock again on a related charge. He was also accused of assaulting Mary Ann Moses, who had tried to come between himself and Margaret Short. Armstrong had then called her 'a long-nosed b_____'. Margaret duly warned him not to use the expression again which admonishment had, of course, served to invite a repetition of the insult. The miner had had to be quick on his feet in order to avoid the shovel that then came flying in his direction. Subsequently, in a show of largesse, Armstrong poured what remained of his whisky over the second Margaret. For this offence he received an additional fine of ten shillings.

Later that year (1875), writing about crimes of violence in the *Durham Chronicle*, Justice Denman showed himself to be one of the few enlightened judges of his day. Looking at the causes of crime he commented:

...Can it be wondered that in densely populated mining villages for instance, where the only institutions are the public-house and the policeman, the vice of intemperance should prevail? In many cases the mining population have no recreation within their reach except what the public-house affords, and for want of innocent resources are now impelled to coarse and brutal pleasures. In the hovels in which too many reside home can have few attractions...

Faced with the temptation of unlimited supplies of beer on the premises, landlords often gave in – and could they drink! In February 1873, Mary Brown, the wife of Robert, landlord of the Red Lion Inn, Winlaton, had her husband summoned for assault. She told the court that on the previous day Brown downed fifty pints, finishing his spree by guzzling an astonishing ten pints in thirty minutes. Expressing their amazement at such a feat, the magistrates ordered the soak to be detained in Gateshead cells for the assault. There Brown suffered a severe attack of the DT's, becoming so violent he had to be watched night and day. Madness followed and he was removed to the county asylum at Sedgefield.

Overconsumption of alcohol was and remains the cause of many premature deaths. William Campbell, popularly known as the Scottish giant, weighed in at 52 stones on his twenty-second birthday in 1878. The landlord of the Duke of Wellington in Newcastle he did not, however, live to celebrate his twenty-third. A doctor, examining him a few months before his death, noted a few statistics and observations in *the Lancet*. William was 6′ 4″ tall with 96″ shoulders and a 76″ chest. When well, his powers of locomotion were considerable. However his fondness for a few jars, which, because of his occupation, were permanently available on tap, was held to be scarcely *likely to be conducive to his health and longevity,* and so it proved.

Although drink was attributed as the direct cause of death of just 496 people in the whole of England and Wales in 1874, alcohol played a large contributory factor in the 223 murders, 1,549 suicides and 11,783 accidental deaths.

Several fiery speakers spoke out against the evils of drink. Tommy Carr, known as the Bishop of Bensham, was a regular orator at Newcastle's Quayside, sparking off several heated debates between imbibers and teetotallers. With many members of the temperance movement being shopkeepers, arguments took the form of the following verbal attack by a countryman:

If them teetotallers had to work like me, they wad syun find whether they cud do wivoot their beer or not. Aall them grocers and butchers are only teetotallers for thor oon intorests

Two dedicated dipso's, who could not do *wivoot their beer* were 60-year-old Thomas Anderson and his 48-year-old wife, Ann. In 1852 Thomas, who travelled the North-East repairing agricultural machinery, rented a room in Walkergate Lane, their third Berwick lodging-house in one month. Telling the coroner's court about their way of life, the mistress of the house related that the couple shared a half-gallon of ale before breakfast and subsequently polished off several bottles of whiskey throughout the day. The Anderson's previous landlady estimated their booze bill at an incredible one sovereign a day. This was financed by a loan obtained against some expensive property they were due to inherit later that year.

35. William Campbell was living proof of the effects of over-imbibing. The landlord was born in Glasgow in 1856 and died at 16, High Bridge, Newcastle in May 1878 weighing 52 stones. He was just 22.

36. The London Hotel in Corstophine Town, long since demolished. More than two-thirds of the arrests in South Shields in 1900 were on drink related charges.

37. Behind the bar in 1882. Pubs were very popular but many parents sent their children out to fetch beer

One night in March, following her normal daily ration Ann, perching on a stool by the fire, complained of feeling slightly indisposed. Leaning back to rest her head on the bed, she promptly collapsed and died. At the post-mortem, held in the workhouse, Dr. Kirkwood stated that death was caused by disease of the heart accelerated by deceased's irregular mode of life. The jury returned a verdict accordingly. It appears that Thomas was averse to drinking alone and duly joined his wife in the big bar in the sky a few days later, following a drunken frenzy.

After their deaths, their total worldly wealth of £1/9/- was possessed by parish officers as a contribution towards burial costs.

ROBBERY IN A BROTHEL AT SUNDERLAND. INFLICTION OF THE 'CAT'.

Thus ran the local headlines in April, 1879. For a number of reasons that may be easily guessed at, bordellos and ale houses were the most dangerous premises in any town. In ports the problems were exacerbated by the thousands of thirsty, sex-starved matelots who made these establishments their second ports of call.

James Lennard, the mate from the schooner 'Sarah of Mistley', agreed terms with 20-year-old Selina Robson in the local in Bishopwearmouth. Back at her place in Charles Street. the couple were soon divesting

themselves. James, at least, was very much up for it but on this occasion the seaman failed to reach the desired naval base. Sarah operated with the help of her accomplice, Thomas Bell, 23, a bully in more ways than one. His habit was to lay in wait for Sarah's drunken punters. Accordingly, he set about James in a cold, merciless manner with copious use of heavy boots and ham-sized fists.

Strong in the arm, the bully satisfied the second half of the saying and was quickly apprehended. He had only been at liberty for one month, following twelve month's inside for a similar offence. Repeat offenders were harshly dealt with and the seven-year sentence he received meant seven years, he would not see the outside world again until he was thirty. He was also to be subjected to twenty strokes of the 'cat'. As corporal punishment of female offenders had long been abolished, Selina was simply sent down for twelve months

38. Ellen Coyle, a 19-year-old prostitute whose height was listed as 4' 9". Most 'ladies of the town' were also convicted for lifting more than their skirts. The watches and wallets of drunken punters were the main targets of many an illicit assignation. Needing to take pride in their appearance, clothes shops were also targeted by doxies and Ellen was convicted, on St Valentine's Day 1873 for 'stealing wearing apparel'.

39. *The old fishing croft near Sandside, Hartlepool c1905. Fisherman held many superstitions about pigs. Police in the town would disguise themselves to mount raids on unlicensed drinking clubs.*

Pubs were probably the most popular pick-up places for prostitutes. Be they foreign sailors, adulterous husbands, inquisitive teenagers or swells slumming it, all punters were greeted with a friendly smile and a fondle in the pockets. Police fought a losing battle against the oldest profession by enforcing laws against landlords for *knowingly permitting their premises to be the habitual resort or place of meeting of suspected prostitutes and allowing them to remain longer than is necessary for the purpose of obtaining reasonable refreshment.*

In other words, like their customers, ladies of the night had to be in and out as quickly as possible with precious little time allowed for relief. Laws containing the words 'knowingly' and 'reasonable' provide some scope for the defence and, with landlords being better off than their customers, many employed lawyers to help them save their licenses. In November, 1873, John Metcalfe, landlord of the Shakespeare Hotel in Hartlepool, stood before the court for allowing doxies to dally in his doorways.

At 8.40 pm one P.C. Huntingdon noticed a drunken prostitute leaving the pub. When ordered to get off the street she promptly obeyed the policeman's instructions and popped back into the Shakespeare for a quickie. Here she was joined by six street-walking sisters. A session certainly looked to be on the cards until the unwelcome intervention of the long arm of the law, in the shape of Sergeant Joyce, who'd appeared to relieve

Constable Huntingdon. Joyce informed Metcalfe about the presence on his premises, for at least half an hour, of the 'unfortunates'. Ten such ladies were duly ejected whilst the landlord protested that he had not known of their patronage.

The Metcalfe case brought the thorny problem of how much time was allowable for 'reasonable refreshment'. There'd be no end of barneys today if landlords refused to serve customers who had been on the premises more than half an hour. Everyone drinks at a different pace, as was pointed out by the defence in this case, over one hundred years ago:

Where one man, or one prostitute, would go into a bar and drink liquor off and be out again, another might stand and chat for a longer time and not drink a larger quantity.

The defence lawyer argued that if the landlord kept filling glass after glass to 'these women' he was

40. *The artist at the Day's Doings certainly had a fertile imagination. Following a heavy gust of wind in March 1871, part of the chimney stack of the Bee Hive pub on Scotswood Road was blown down. Fears and rumours of an earthquake quickly spread and inebriates squeezed through all available exits.*

FALL OF A CHIMNEY AT NEWCASTLE-UPON-TYNE.—EXCITING INCIDENT RESULTING FROM THE EARTHQUAKE PANIC.

obviously breaking the law, but he determined to call witnesses who would testify this was not the case. In retrospect it seems a rather strange society which allowed boys of 11 to serve behind the bar, but which banned adult women from drinking in a public house for more than half an hour. But such was the norm in Hartlepool, and indeed in Britain as a whole during the 1870s.

One of the witnesses called in the defence of John Metcalfe was his 11-year-old son, also called 'John'. John junior had been serving on the night in question. He told the court that five women came in at about 9 pm and ordered only one and a half' pence worth of drink each. Other locals backed up this story: the ladies had only consumed a small amount of beer and had only been present for a short period of time. Despite this evidence, however, Metcalfe lost the case. He was fined £3 for knowingly having prostitutes on his premises for longer than was necessary for their 'reasonable refreshment'. His license was not, however, endorsed.

In the same court William Sewell, the landlord of the Oddfellow's Arms, was fined 5/6d for serving a quart of beer after hours. The victim of recently introduced licensing hours, Sewell had served a customer twenty minutes after the 11 pm deadline. His defence didn't say much for the speed of service in the Oddfellow's: Sewell had been serving beer ordered an hour and twenty minutes earlier.

Quite what was going through Philip Fitzgerald's head on an autumn evening in Durham in 1875 may never be known; he certainly wouldn't remember. At 9.15 on the night in question he knocked at the police-station door in a state of Brahms and Liszt. Swaying but speechless, he was immediately received by a kind policemen who found him a room for the extortionate rate of five shillings the night, which sum he duly paid in court. A rare case of being drunk but not disorderly.

Those who could drink and control themselves were, on occasions, leniently treated. In 1873 the landlord of the Lord Nelson Inn, Sandgate, along with his brother-in-law, was summoned on a charge of being drunk in his public-house. The police raided the pub at 11.30 pm and found the two men well plastered. Mr Joel, defending, put forward a simple but compelling argument on behalf of his clients. He pleaded that if other people had the privilege of getting drunk in their own houses, then so too did a landlord, especially after business hours. The lawyer stressed the fact that his clients had created no disturbance nor otherwise broken the law. The judge seemed to agree, ordering the defendants to pay costs only. Neither was fined.

Most of those accused of drunkenness pleaded guilty. Self-deluders who denied the charge fitted into three categories: the mad, the sad and the ingenious. Exactly which category Mrs Ann Fagan fell into the reader must decide. Brought to trial in Hartlepool 1874, her case reveals the typically brutish sexual relations existing between husbands and wives whose sole pleasure was ale:

Police Constable Pudney said that on Saturday night, at half-past ten o'clock, the defendant was drunk in

Back Church-street. He told her to go away and she would not, but kept cursing and swearing. Sergeant Forster also said the woman was drunk, he had to help her along.

DEFENDANT: I was standing at my own back door. I was not drunk, but confused at being taken away without a cause. I had had one glass of ale for dinner and only that during the day. When my husband came in, he made a disturbance on the stairs, and I thought it best to keep out of the way, so I went to the back door.

A neighbour deposed that she was advising the defendant to keep out of the house, until the husband's passion went off, when the policeman dragged her away. She was not under the influence of drink.

Sergeant White was in the station when defendant was brought in. She could not get into the cell without staggering along the wall. She was drunk.

Mrs Fagan was fined 5/- and ordered to pay costs of 6/4d.

In Wagga-Wagga (West Hartlepool) police resorted to disguising themselves as navvies in order to raid unlicensed premises. As the result of one of these raids an elderly widow, Hannah Joyce, was arrested and brought before the bench. The report of the trial provides fascinating reading:

Sergeant Wilkinson and Constable Buck, on Tuesday night, were disguised as working men, for the purpose of detecting the defendant who was suspected of selling beer at her house in Florence-street, Wagga-Wagga. They saw several women go to the house with tin cans. They quietly followed one woman into the back-yard, and waited at the door to see what passed. They were rewarded by seeing the woman receive a quart of beer in a tin, from the defendant, who received in payment a coin which she held up to the light and showed to be a sixpence.

The officers then made their appearance. The customer threw down her can and bolted and the defendant struck the sergeant in the face with what proved to be a door key. In the house was an 18-gallon cask half-full of beer, also a bottle containing beer.

MR BELL (for the defence): Didn't Mrs Joyce say she was going to warm the beer for her own use?

SERGEANT WILKINSON: No, and besides there was no fire in the house. (laughter).

Buck said he was dressed as a navvy. Next morning, when he served the summons, defendant said : "If they had been some of your men, I wouldn't have cared, but for two navvies to come it was badly using me! For the defence, Mr Bell called a lodger, who declared that the beer belonged to him and others, and that Mrs Joyce had no interest in it at all. He also called Mary Kelly, the woman who was said to have purchased the beer, but she, being in what is considered an 'interesting' condition, declined to be sworn, in obedience to an Irish superstition that an oath taken during pregnancy will bring a curse upon the child.

Hannah Joyce was fined £20 with costs!

41. Police were often called to pubs because inebriates refused to leave the premises. There was a good chance the evicting officers had partaken of a few beverages themselves.

By the turn of the century other forms of entertainment were becoming popular, though a large hardcore of serious drinkers continued to make nuisances of themselves. The black-listing of habitual drunkards was introduced with varying degrees of success. Photographs and descriptions of perpetual offenders were distributed to pubs whose landlords were heavily fined if caught selling liquor to the serial drinkers.

A dipso from Blakewell Road, Tweedmouth, Berwick, Jane Virtue didn't live up to her name. After being spotted in a drunken state in the Tweed Tavern, Jane was turned out by P.C.Smith, who warned her that if she visited another public-house she would be locked up. After popping into the chippy, Jane disregarded the advice, staggered into the King's Head and was promptly arrested. Upon arrival at the police station, Jane collapsed and was put into a cell to sleep off the effects of a drink or ten too many.

The Chief Constable told the court that Jane had been convicted three times within the previous twelve months; once for being drunk on licensed premises; once for being drunk in charge of a child, and the third time for being drunk and disorderly.

Jane apologised to the court and told the bench that it would be for the best if they black-listed her. Her wish was granted, along with a fine of 40/- or 21 days imprisonment.

42a

eventually found a further month's accommodation over the Christmas period and her cheerful likeness was displayed in the hostelries over the next three years.

In the same court, on the same day, a labourer, Edward Murphy, denied being drunk when he was arrested. The doctor's evidence shows as much about the general level of education of the time as it does about Edward's degree of intoxication. After stating that the man could walk without swaggering and sign his name *in a tolerably fair hand, probably as good as he could today* the doctor answered questions from the bench:

Dr. GEURLEY: *He was sober: he did not look at all 'muzzy'. When asked the name of the month (it was November) the defendant said it was September but then corrected himself; and as to the day, he said it was the 9th and then the 10th. But if you were to ask a dozen people among the crowd behind here, what month it is I don't suppose they could tell you.*

Edward was fined 10/- with costs.

Offences relating to drugs other than alcohol were as rare as those influenced by the demon drink were common. One of the few mentioned in newspapers, a crime ahead of its time, was brought against Annie Bailey of Whitley Bay in 1908. In a portend of the late twentieth switch from alcohol to drug related crime, Annie was charged with obtaining goods under false pretences to feed her habit. Her husband told the court that she had been addicted to morphine for ten years and was now even stealing from their children.

A TROUBLESOME WOMAN

42

Elizabeth Beech of 28, Golden Square, Berwick-Upon-Tweed was put on the black list of habitual drunkards following three arrests for being drunk and disorderly in 1913. She had spent a month inside for each offence. When apprehended for the fourth time, in Marygate, an officer saw her ringing a hotel bell and quickly making off into the darkness. Elizabeth

43. Language has certainly changed over the centuries but has behaviour? This illustration from Newcastle in 1870 was published under the headline 'The Gay Deceiver'. William Murdock was off for a little hanky-panky with the new love in his life when the couple were spotted by an old flame.

THE GAY DECEIVER'

The inhabitants of Newcastle enjoyed seeing a pair of toffs get their come-uppance. How they must have chuckled when they read about the 'gay deceiver' and his rich, brassy wench.

William Murdock and the new love in his life, Miss Kearsley, a young lady of considerable personal attractions, were promenading in their best attire along the High Street in September 1870. The weather was fine but in the space of five seconds the pair were saturated from head to foot. Water had been deliberately poured over their heads by a lady from the window of a nearby house. Besides being dirty, the water was hot, and one side of the young man's face, and the neck and shoulders of his companion, were severely scolded. A brush, flannel and soap also rained down on the unsuspecting couple.

William and Miss Kearsley were off for a little how's your Father at a friend's house, but the soaking quickly cooled their ardour. Murdock recognised the woman who stood at the window, hands on hips, letting out a raucous belly laugh. He issued a warrant against her and they next met in court where the Miss Shower Puss revealed her motives. She had been engaged to Murdock for three and a half years and then dumped when a richer model, in the shape of Miss Kearsley, arrived on the scene.

Who could control themselves when presented with such an opportunity? The jilted Jane pleaded her case with such eloquence that the magistrate discharged her when she agreed to keep the peace.

Domestic disputes were not confined to the poorer classes. Because of the respectable positions of the two Darlings the proceedings at Durham Police Court in 1869 quickly became the talk of the town.

Henry James Darling, of Waddington Street, Durham was charged with having unlawfully assaulted and beaten his wife without cause. As we shall see, however, Mary Troutbeck Darling was fully capable of giving as good as she got.

Let's join the packed courtroom where evidence has already been given that Henry Darling was *a little on the go* and had taken *a little too much refreshment*. Coming downstairs Henry noticed his wife removing the table-cloth. This he promptly seized, screwed into a ball and pitched into the passage. He then ordered his wife out of the room, 'rudely' pinched her and then struck a backhanded blow across her chest. Mary Troutbeck Darling was the first to answer questions:

Q: *How long have you been married to your husband?*
A: *Eleven months on Tuesday.*
Q: *On Friday night, about 6 o'clock were you preparing tea?*
A: *Yes, I was taking the cover off the table.*
Q: *Was defendant in the room at the time?*
A: *Yes, he came down whilst I was taking the cover off the table.*
Q: *What did he say?*
A: *He told me to take the table-cover to my uncle's, Mr Douthwaite's* (Laughter).
Q: *I suppose that's a figurative expression for a pawnbroker.*
A: *Yes Sir, Mr Douthwaite is a pawnbroker I believe.*

Q: *What did he next do or say?*
A: *He told me I was to leave his sitting room. But I told him I could not do so as I was going to get my tea and there was no other room in the house.*
Q: *What did he do after that?*
A: *He followed me around the room and got hold of me to put me out. I would not go out. He pinched me on the left arm and struck me on the chest with his elbows.*

Mrs Darling then added that her husband had ill-used her from the day they married. Under cross-examination from the defence, however, a rather different version as to who wore the trousers in the household was to emerge, much to the amusement of the court audience.

Q: *Did you ever strike him?*
A: *Not till after he had struck at me. I was compelled to strike in self defence.*
Q: *Have you got a pair of 'taws'* [a leather strap split into strips at the end] (Laughter).
A: *There is such a thing in the house.*
Q: *What are they like?*
A: *They are made of leather to be sure.* (Laughter).
Q: *What length are they?* (Laughter).
A: *I cannot tell.*
Q: *Have you ever used these 'taws' to your husband?*
A: *I beg your pardon. I won't answer your question.* (Laughter).
Q: *Now, upon your oath, have you not used the 'taws' to your husband on several occasions?* (Laughter) *On the Friday night in question?*
A: *He ordered me out and then I struck him.* (Laughter).
Q: *Did you lay them on well?* (Laughter).
A: *No.*
Q: *Didn't you mark his face?*
A: *No I did not.*

An embarrassed and furious Mrs Darling then left the stand to be replaced by her servant who told the court:

I have seen many quarrels between my master and mistress… I think blows have passed between them on about six different occasions. I do not remember anything about a cribbage board and a pipe being knocked out of my master's hand and mouth. She took the 'taws' to him after he had struck at her…I don't know whether Mrs Darling kept the 'taws' to whip the cats (Laughter). *I know there's no children in the house.*

On the day in question the servant added:

She hit her husband on the shoulders: not over the face. He did not take his whipping very quietly. (Laughter).

Mr Darling, who seemed to have suffered enough for his drunken rage, was fined a further five shillings. The audience thoroughly enjoyed their afternoon's entertainment.

THE ASSAULT CASE AT DURHAM

44. The Darlings were not as lovey-dovey as their name suggests. Their honeymoon period did not last long as, less than a year after marriage, the Durham couple were at each other's throats. Henry used his fists and verbal intimidation, Mary took the 'taws' into her own hands.

45. *Picking clothes outside a provisions dealer, probably in the Walker area of Newcastle. There was a ready market for second-hand and stolen clothes and you weren't always guaranteed to find your washing pegged up on the line where you had left it.*

A QUARRELSOME OLD COUPLE

Insights into daily life and the colourful language employed between husband and wife is especially well illustrated when court reporters resort to relating their stories phonetically. Such was the case in *The Sunderland Echo* in March, 1865:

Thomas Mason, an elderly miner, was charged with assaulting Mary Mason, his wife, who was also old and *so narvish*, as she herself put it, that she could not tell her story straight. She said her husband got drunk twice on the Saturday – the first time before dinner, when he usually commenced to *argey* and aggravate her.

"An he hez the aggravationest tongue that ivver was in a man's mouth – he hez whizzivver."

Every Saturday, Thomas got drunk, came home for dinner, went to bed and after tea went out to get drunk a second time. After that he was usually mischievous. Three weeks previously, when he'd come home, Mary had told him that supper was on the table. Instead of sitting down to get it, however, he kicked her off the "cracket", a stool upon which she had been sitting. She shouted for assistance and was comforted by the neighbours.

DEFENDANT: *"She us a varry bad tongue, an 'aw pushed the steul an 'her ower together – a nivver laid a finger on her. She has ivverything sent into the house tin her, an' she hez nowt te de but eat her meat."*

MR ANDERSON: *"But you get drunk twice every Saturday?"*

DEFENDANT: *"No, no; aw whiles get a little sup, ye knaw."*

The bench bound the old man over to keep the peace.

On a more serious note domestic disputes were so common that the odd black eye or bruise was rarely reported. Unfortunately some attacks were far more serious. Unemployed men whose wives or girlfriends had moved back to live with their parents harboured deep grudges and, when tanked up, the abandoned spouses would sometimes seek out the women whom they felt had deserted them.

In 1885, all was going well for pitman Thomas Smith and Edith Dyer, who had lived together in Sunderland for 12 months. Disaster was looming, however, for that year the miner lost his job. Following the advice of Edith's mother, the couple sold their worldly goods. Edith quickly followed table and chairs, leaving the unemployed young man to brood over his change of fortune and furniture.

A few days later, seething with pent up anger and resentment, Smith was spotted lurking outside the Dyer's home in Hetton. Forcing his way in the unemployed collier set about slashing at the throats of the three female members of the household. Pursuing the fleeing Edith to a neighbour's home, the demented knife-man would surely have killed her had assistance not arrived.

Charged with attempted triple murder, Smith's lawyer told the court that his client had been happy before losing his job and greatly resented his mother-in-law, who had caused his Edith to leave him. A plea for clemency on the grounds that Smith was acting under an aberration was rejected and the poor man was sent down for seven years.

Many men wouldn't take 'no' for an answer, imposing their unwanted attentions on the objects of their desire with sometimes fatal consequences. 19-year-old Elizabeth Clementson had been separated from her husband for eighteen months. In November 1869 she was to be found living with her parents at 95, Hinde Street, Scotswood Road. But Elizabeth was destined to become the victim of a Victorian 'stalker', a man who had been charged with assaulting her and bailed at £20.

Robert Macdonald, a labourer from Railway Terrace was infatuated with the teenager and could not, or would not, keep away from her. Elizabeth made out a deposition as to what had happened to her shortly before she died. Read out to a hushed coroner's court, the gist of her statement was as follows:

On Saturday the 3rd of October, about three o'clock in the afternoon, Elizabeth was in the house of Peter Carty, on Tyne Street, Scotswood Road. Robert Macdonald and three other young men came in, one of whom had half a gallon of ale in his hand. Macdonald went into the bedroom where Elizabeth was chatting with Mrs Carty and a young woman named Kitty McCourt. Macdonald gave Kitty a slap across the face and then left the room. The three outraged women followed him into the kitchen where he again struck the hapless Miss McCourt. Elizabeth bravely told him to let the young woman alone. Macdonald responded by asking what it had to do with her and then punched her behind her left ear. She retaliated by grabbing a poker and crying *I won't take that for nothin*. He then gripped her by the neck and someone took the poker from her. Macdonald let rip a torrent of abusive language at Elizabeth who, in order to escape him, fled into the bedroom. Sometime afterwards Macdonald pursued her and seized hold of her *by the lower part of the body*, whilst making lewd suggestions.

Some four weeks later Elizabeth was examined by a doctor following a series of headaches. There were no external marks of violence upon the head but an abscess was discovered behind the left ear. This was the result of an untreated injury to the bone. Elizabeth died a few days after the medical examination.

The post-mortem revealed some surprises. Dr. Hume told the coroner's court that he had examined the body internally and thought that disease of the lungs was the immediate cause of death, though this was secondary to the abscess. Whilst the doctor acknowledged that a blow to the head had been inflicted, he could not say when the blow had taken place. The coroner's jury was not so reticent and delivered the verdict *that the deceased died from disease of the lungs, accelerated by the blow received from Robert Macdonald.*

The coroner made out a warrant for the committal of Robert Macdonald on the charge of manslaughter. Once again bail was allowed. At his subsequent trial the case against Macdonald was dismissed as it was considered that the blow he struck had not been responsible for Elizabeth's death.

Northumberland County Constabulary.

AMENDED POLICE INFORMATION.

MANSLAUGHTER.

Wanted on a Coroner's Warrant for the Manslaughter of his wife Elizabeth Dewar, at Alnwick on the 14th JULY, 1893.

ALEXANDER DEWAR *alias* SCOTT,

Age 43. Height, 5ft. 5 or 6in., stoutish build ; Hair grey, Moustache light, turning grey, no whiskers ; Nose a little twisted to one side ; walks slightly lame from an accident ; Native of Glasgow, is much addicted to drink ; by trade a plasterer, but sometimes in the winter months makes his living by playing the Violin in the streets and public-houses.

DEWAR has for the past few months been working at his trade about MORPETH which place he left on the 12th, inst. by train for Newcastle, he is very unsettled and never stays long in one place. He has been a member of the Alnwick Militia, has likewise been a member of the Dumfries Militia in the name of Alexander Scott, from which regiment he was discharged about 4 years ago; when last seen was dressed in a brown coat white cotton or linen jacket underneath, brown vest moleskin trousers, and grey cap with one peak.

It is earnestly requested that immediate search and enquiry be made for the above described person, and if found to arrest, or should any trace be found to wire Captain H. D. TERRY, Chief Constable, Morpeth, or to myself,

ANDREW RUTHERFORD, Superintendent.

POLICE OFFICE, ALNWICK, 21st JULY, 1893.

JOHN DAVISON, PRINTER, ST. MICHAEL'S PANT, ALNWICK.

46. Police wanted poster. Despite the lack of a photograph, the written description painted a comprehensive picture and Dewar was arrested in South Shields by an eagle-eyed policeman one week later.

In the absence of today's technology, police and public alike were provided with very detailed written accounts of suspects on the wanted list. These proved surprisingly effective and many a villain was apprehended because of details like, *a nose, a little twisted to one side* or *a predilection for playing the fiddle*.

On 15th July, 1893 an inquest was held at Alnwick Workhouse into the death of Elizabeth Dewar. A resident of Clayport Street, she had been admitted with her two children (10 and 5) the previous Tuesday. Elizabeth, tended by her anxious 17-year-old daughter, had arrived in an omnibus. She was very ill and complained of pains all over her body, her stomach being particularly sore. On her deathbed she made the following deposition:

I am the wife of Brian Alexander Dewar and live in Clayport. He is a plasterer. He has been working in Morpeth. He came here on 24th. June. Between 8 and 9 he came in the worse of drink. He is a passionate man. He asked me where I had been. I told him. He struck me and knocked me down with a kick. He struck me several times. Once he struck me on the bowels. On the following day he was again the worse of drink. At night about half-past-eight he struck me again. He went away on Sunday by the last train. I felt unwell on Tuesday or Wednesday and sent for Dr. White. I have been unwell ever since.

When asked to sign her deposition all she could

manage was *Alnwick*, being too ill to add Elizabeth Dewar. Cause of death was entered as peritonitis.

Police then questioned the couple's 10-year-old daughter who said that though Dewar was not drunk, neither was he sober, *he had drink in him*. The Saturday night beating followed false allegations that his wife had been drinking whereas, in fact, she had been to a friend's to help with the mangling. The daughter witnessed her mother being repeatedly punched and kicked until the intervention of a neighbour at 10. 30 pm. The neighbour later testified that he saw Dewar swear and call his wife ugly names but did not see him strike her. In his opinion Dewar was the worse for drink; his wife was sober.

There was enough evidence to issue a wanted poster. With Dewar being an itinerant, details were circulated far and wide. One ended up on the notice board at South Shields police station. The very week after its release the poster produced results. On a Saturday afternoon a Police Inspector was eyeballing a rather dishevelled-looking stranger in King Street. Their eyes met. The policeman was still reflecting as to where he had seen him before when the man approached, introduced himself, and asked if he was looking for him? Dewar said that he was tired of walking about and, having heard rumours that he was on the wanted list, determined to give himself up. He was wearing the same clothes as in the police description and had made no attempt to disguise himself.

Dewar did not know that his wife had died and when so informed, burst into tears and appeared to be genuinely grief-stricken.

When told of the allegations against him he sought to defend himself with a twisted kind of logic. He insisted that he had never struck his wife on the body, he had merely beaten her about the head. When arrested he was adamant:

I admit blacking her eye but no kicking. We were quite friendly on the Sunday morning and she cooked dinner and we parted good friends on Sunday night.

Charged with manslaughter, Dewar defended himself. He set out to prove that his wife was a drunken waster and bad mother, implying that she needed a good kicking from time to time to make her realise her responsibilities to himself and the children. The jury were, as ever, all male. Dewar argued that he travelled the country seeking employment and returned with money to buy the children food and clothes. He accused his wife of wasting money on drink and not sending the children to school.

In a world where it was common for children to be sent out for beer and spirits, the Dewars were no exception. Here Dewar (D) questions his ten-year-old daughter (W) as to the events on the Sunday he left home:

D: *Did I send you for a drink of beer?*
W: *Yes.*
D: *Your mother had a drink of it?*
W: *Yes.*
D: *Did she ask me to send for a glass of whisky?*
W: *I don't remember.*
D: *Did you go for one? Don't you remember going for a glass of whisky for your mother?*

The daughter denied buying any spirits for her mother but Dewar kept badgering her in a lengthy line of questioning that gave the impression that she was lying. A far more intelligent man than might be expected, Dewar sought to prove that his wife's bodily injuries could have been caused by a drunken fall. He sought leave to call his son, then serving on the training ship 'Wellesley', as a character reference, but the boy failed to show.

Found guilty of manslaughter, Dewar was sentenced to eight months with hard labour.

Many men walked from the courts, or served ludicrously light sentences for manslaughter because doctors testified that husbands' violence was not the direct cause of death. In cases of domestic fatality it appears that men were only convicted of murder if they shot or slashed their partners.

When a wilful murder charge was thrown out by a Grand Jury in 1875, 42-year-old labourer John Tully from West Hartlepool was tried for the lesser crime of grievous bodily harm. Throughout his trial no end of witnesses testified as to Tully's sadistic behaviour towards his wife, Bridget. One neighbour testified that on 15th March he'd found Tully with a poker about to strike his wife, who was lying on the floor, her hair tightly entwined in her husband's free hand. Tully then kicked her in the abdomen.

The next day, after hearing loud piercing screams, another neighbour discovered Bridget bleeding profusely from the mouth. That same night both her eyes were blackened and a fresh bruise appeared on her nose. The Tully's 15-year-old daughter testified seeing her mother smashed against a wall while other witnesses related what the defendant did with his heavy boots.

Bridget Tulley died a week after the March beating and, surprise, surprise, the expert refused to attribute her death to any of the injuries she sustained on that occasion. Found guilty of assault, the dead woman's husband received the paltry sentence of nine months.

Not all husbands took their boots or fists to erring wives. In 1883, when a miner's wife, aged forty-two summers, ran off with the family's 25-year-old lodger, the abandoned spouse responded in a manner as easygoing as his wife literally was, indeed he seems almost philosophical: *If she cares more for him than me, let her gan: I can seun get another.*

THE MILKMAN AND THE PORK BUTCHER'S WIFE

47. If maids fell pregnant they would be dismissed losing not only their job but their living accommodation as well. Many resorted to back-street abortions which were often botched. Others simply pretended they were not in the family way and gave birth single-handedly. In 1870 a maid, Mary Ann Robinson, living in Gateshead, gave birth in her first floor bedroom and promptly threw her baby out of the window. At her resulting trial for infanticide she was deemed to be of unsound mind at the time of the offence and found not guilty.

Courts were intimidating places for women. The Mayor of South Shields argued that dogs had to wear muzzles and so too should quarrelsome women who talked too much. Superintendent Richardson agreed. Given these entrenched misogynistic attitudes, many women were reluctant to report sexual attacks, and cases coming to court were doubtless a small fraction of those that took place.

The victims of sex attacks today rightly complain that they are abused and shamed twice: once in the original attack and the second time at court. One can only imagine the stress women suffered in the Victorian courtroom where judge, jury and legal representatives were all male. Many cases were thrown out as, for one trivial reason or another, the men in court considered that the victim had consented to sex. The following case from Morpeth, 1847, was typical.

John Charlton (33) was charged with feloniously assaulting Rachel Weddell on Sunday, 4th October. Rachel was a watchmaker's servant and, during the afternoon, whilst the family were away, Charlton appeared at the house ostensibly to leave his watch for repair. On the pretext of further wishing to have his name engraved on it, he followed Rachel into the kitchen where, according to her testimony, 'he twice attempted to commit, or did

commit, a rape upon her.' Mr Granger for the defence argued that the girl who was, after all, only a mere servant, had consented and the all-male jury agreed. On this occasion at least Charlton did not go down.

In the same year, with the evidence against him irrefutable, 54-year-old Archibald Pattison was transported for life for raping a 71-year-old woman in a field. Cases like this were however, rare, the tendency being to treat convicted sex offenders leniently, particularly by today's standards and especially when the offence was against a prostitute or pauper.

In 1874 five youths were charged with aggravated assault on Jane Ball. She had arrived in Hartlepool just a few days previously and, finding herself penniless, had little choice but to sleep rough. Having asked an old man known as 'Stockton Martin' to show her the way to Town Moor, she bedded herself down in the field at about 10 pm. Unfortunately, unbeknown to either party, Jane and her guide had been followed by five drunken youths. Once the old man had departed, the louts pounced on Jane, pinning her to the ground while the ringleader, Cairns, committed *an abominable outrage upon her*.

A sentence of six months hard labour was imposed on two of the gang while the other three got one month each, the usual sentence for the theft of a handkerchief.

With much hanky-panky going on between master and servant, unwanted sexual advances would normally be brushed aside with a few forceful words of rejection. It took outsiders to challenge the norm. When a case of indecent assault came to court in Durham, 1870, it might well have been due to the fact that the married complainant was of German origin and would not be deterred from bringing the action. The accused, John Reid, a former teacher turned milkman, should have kept his sex drive bottled up; instead he turned it on the hapless Bertha Hind. In the absence of witnesses to the assault the onus fell upon the magistrate and recorder to determine who was telling the truth.

Bertha Hind's story was that Reid called in at the pork-butcher's in New Elvet at approximately 6 pm on 10th September to deliver milk. Mrs Hind was in the shop by herself at the time, holding her baby in her arms. Dipping behind the counter she picked up a jug to receive the milk but, noticing it was tea-stained, she asked the defendant to hold her baby whilst she rinsed it out. The report continued that Reid *seized hold of her in the middle of the body and behaved himself in a very rude manner,* which would indicate that the milkman had jugs of a different kind on his mind. A master of the double-entendre the reporter wrote, *Mrs Hind refused to take his milk and the defendant left the shop with a smile on his face.* Two hours later, knowing she would not be there, Reid returned and left the milk.

On the following Monday an enraged pork-butcher went to John Reid's farm in Halgarth Street with the intention of adding certain parts of the dairyman's anatomy to his mince. With Reid absent on his rounds, his wife and daughter took the full brunt of the German butcher's verbal attack. He told her that if her husband had no control over his *animal or goatish propensities* he should leave the parish of St. Oswald's and go to Salt Lake City and Brigham Young would give him plenty of employment in Utah!

In court defence argued that it would be highly improbable that their client would commit such an act in a shop open to the gaze of every passer-by. They added that Mrs Hind had not told her husband of the groping until several hours later, implying that the 'assault' was therefore a figment of her imagination and that the whole case was therefore very suspicious. After a short consultation with counsel, the recorder stated that despite the evidence not being as clear as they would like, the court held that an assault had taken place and a fine of 20s and costs was imposed.

Just one month later three short reports, one after the other, also appeared in the *Durham Chronicle.* They say much about the value placed upon women in Victorian times. They are quoted in their entirety:

BESTIALITY AT TOW LAW

John Corrigan (46) pitman, was charged with bestiality at Tow Law, on the 10th of July. Mr Meynell prosecuted and Mr Blackwell defended the prisoner. He was found guilty and sentenced to two years' imprisonment hard labour.

RAPE AT HOUGHTON-LE-SPRING

Ralph Pearson (20) pitman, was indicted for committing a rape upon Elizabeth Thompson at Houghton-le-Spring, on the 6th August. Mr Meyell appeared for the prosecution, and Mr Blackwell defended the prisoner. The jury found the prisoner guilty and he was sentenced to 15 months' imprisonment.

SODOMY AT SUNDERLAND

John Hind (20) sailor, was charged with sodomy at Sunderland on the 16th September 1870. Mr Able prosecuted, the prisoner was not defended. He was found guilty and sentenced to 15 years' penal servitude.

SUFFER THE LITTLE CHILDREN

48. The shame of having a baby out of wedlock resulted in thousands of botched abortions and babies being murdered or abandoned by their mothers shortly after birth.

A clip round the ear for minor offences and a belting or caning for more serious misdemeanours was accepted as the norm by most Victorian children. Some parents,

49 and 50. Sentences in rape cases varied according to the social status of the victim. Some women knew how best to defend themselves without going to court.

BRUTAL ASSAULT ON A LADY.

SHE KICKED HIM BELOW THE BELT.

51. Hartlepool again c.1906. A typical scene with a housewife scrubbing the doorstep and a young lad walking barefoot.

usually when slewed, went far too far and inflicted punishments bordering on the sadistic. In a world which regarded women and children as, at best, second class citizens, courts were not child friendly and indeed many elderly magistrates enthusiastically supported the chastisement of children. Even when convicted, abusive parents faced sentences not much higher than those imposed on fare-dodgers, who avoided paying for train tickets.

In June 1873 at Stockton Police Court Edward Cuthbert was charged with an aggravated assault on his 12-year-old daughter at their room in Beaumont Street. When Cuthbert heard that the child had been charged with stealing a pair of boots, the labourer devised his own particular punishment. Tying his daughter, clad only in a chemise, to the bed-post he then fastened a walking stick beneath her knees and bound her legs and arms together. After giving her an introductory stroke with a birch rod, he left her shivering in this torturous posture for the rest of the night.

Cuthbert returned at six the following morning and, with the poor girl still tightly bound, laid into her again for a further half-an-hour. His parental diligence was rewarded with a mere two months.

As with most other offences, the sentencing of paedophiles was entirely inconsistent. 26-year-old

Frederick Baker was convicted on a charge of criminal assault in Sunderland, 1885. His victim was a four-year-old girl whom he had enticed, along with her younger brother, with the promise of *pretty things*, to go with him into a timber yard where the offence took place.

Despite the fact that the assault was witnessed by some local lads, Baker pleaded 'not guilty'. The defence disgracefully suggested two reasons for the infant's injuries: that they were caused by an accident sustained whilst she was playing on pit props heaped up on the dockside, or that they may have been the result of scarlet fever!

In a classic case of understatement the judge described the offence as *horrible* and sentenced Baker to two years' imprisonment which, he said, was the maximum penalty the law allowed.

52. Street urchins receiving a good ticking off in Wrangham's Railway, between City Road and Sandgate, Newcastle. Then, as now, youngsters were responsible for many of the crimes perpetrated. In their defence, at least hungry children of the times stole to feed themselves, not a drug habit.

The incidence of abuse against children occurring within the family home, committed by relatives or 'friends' was far more prevalent than attacks upon children by strangers. And once again the sentences imposed for such offences seem fairly light by today's standards. In the parish of Cornhill in 1873, watchmaker Robert Leck pleaded guilty to assaulting Agnes Arries, a girl under ten years of age, *with intent to carnally know and abuse her.* The victim was his granddaughter. Leck was sent down for ten months.

Throughout the country death and childbirth went hand in hand and very little interest was shown when infant corpses were discovered. Such discoveries merited little comment as this typical newspaper report, from 1873 shows:

The dead body of a male child eight weeks old has been found in a field near Monkseaton near Shields and medical evidence proves that it died from want and exposure.

One of the most underreported crimes of Victorian times was the wilful killing by mothers of their children. This usually happened shortly after birth but could occur at any age when a woman could no longer cope.

In 1846 Margaret Stoker was charged with drowning her 14-month-old baby daughter near Castle Eden. On the way to Durham gaol she confided in her escort:

Oh Sir, I hope they will be canny with me as it is the first thing I have done.

A policeman later testified:

When I searched the house I found a halfpenny, a thimble and a piece of net. When she was before the coroner she desired to see the body of her child. She saw it, she said 'my canny, canny bairn what made me do this to you? Many a weary foot we have wandered'. She embraced and kissed the child. I had some difficulty in getting her away from the body.

Margaret was sentenced to death but the judge recommend mercy.

Cases of murder, infanticide, manslaughter and cruelty against children, mostly by their parents, were coming before the courts every week. Mary Ann Robinson a servant living in Grosvenor Street, Gateshead, gave birth unaided in her first floor bedroom in 1870. She then promptly threw the child out of the window.

A concerned neighbour sent for a doctor but the baby died a short time later. At her trial for infanticide, the defence argued that their client was of weak intellect and had committed the offence whilst she was *unsound of mind.* The jury returned a verdict of not guilty.

Just how brutish life could be in the inner cities is illustrated by another manslaughter charge brought to the court above. John Carr returned from work to find his supper not fully prepared. A furious row resulted in Mrs Carr gathering her children and taking them out

53. Newcastle street life. The male in the photo would probably have needed some of the Hudson's soap to wash his feet at the end of the day. A photo taken in all innocence that has sinister overtones today.

into the street. Incensed, the angry husband picked up the nearest available weapon, a pair of tongs, and in his pent-up rage threw them with great force at his wife. The tongs struck their young daughter, Elizabeth, on the head. She died eight days later from the resulting injury. Finding him guilty of manslaughter, the judge took a very lenient view of Mr Carr's predicament, saying that the death had been an accident. Carr was sentence to one day's imprisonment.

In September 1909, 19-year-old Dorothy Harrison reported for duty as a general maid at the Brittannia Inn in Cleadon. Her employer, Mrs Ellison, later stated that Dorothy looked unwell but this did not deter the landlady from instructing her new servant to share a bedroom with her own 8-year-old son. That night, as the boy slept, Dorothy gave birth, anxiously stifling her screams and groans. Her main concern was not to alert the household to the bloody event taking place in the early hours.

At 7.30 the next morning the young servant was spotted carrying a blood-stained bundle into the yard. She shuffled to the pigsty behind the loo and returned empty-handed. Following a search by other members of the household, the body of a new-born child was discovered. When Mrs Ellison was informed of this fact, a further search of the servant's bed revealed large blood stains and other incriminating evidence. The police were called and Dorothy was transferred to the infirmary where it was confirmed that she had recently given birth. More damningly for her, it was also confirmed that the baby had had a separate existence, had drawn breath but had been suffocated by a handkerchief tightly wedged into its mouth.

When told that she was to be charged with the wilful murder of her child the young servant replied: *I did not know what I was doing.*

The defence argued that Dorothy was so afraid of being discovered through the baby's crying that she had silenced it with the handkerchief. Dorothy was convicted of concealment of birth and bound over to be of good behaviour.

BABES IN THE WOOD

Compared with other young women, Isabella Young, the happily-married wife of a papermaker, was well provided for. Young and healthy, with a beautiful young family, she appeared to have everything to live for. But all was not as it seemed.

At 3 pm one summer's afternoon in Durham, 1872, Isabella left home with two of her children. Leaving the baby girl in her perambulator by the road, she took the elder child, later described as *a pretty girl,* into the woods where Isabella produced a dinner knife and attempted to slash her daughter's throat. The little girl fought off her deranged mother and rushed home, her clothes saturated in blood.

Isabella then returned to the baby and stabbed her before slitting her own throat from ear to ear. Two passing men, hearing cries from the woods, discovered the bloody carnage. The mother was obviously dead but the baby, despite having been stabbed in the stomach, was expected to live.

A coroner's jury returned the verdict *that the deceased had cut her throat while in an unsound state of mind.*

TRAGEDY AT (BLACKHILL) DURHAM

54. Suffering from melancholy, Isabella Young took her two daughters to Blackhill and attempted to murder them both before slashing her own throat. Remarkably both children survived but the distressed mother had bled to death before discovery by two passersby, who were attracted by the baby's crying.

55

56

57

55. 14-year-old Stephen Monaghan was sentenced to ten days with hard labour for stealing money in 1873. Of more concern to the wee (4' 6") Scottish lad was the adjoinder to his sentence - three years at Market Weighton Reformatory.

56. 5-year-old Margaret Cash dressed in her summer best. Fashion conscious, she was sentenced to two month's hard labour for stealing a coat.

57. 15-year-old Patrick Garraty appears to have lost his hair at a very young age. He was sent down for one month for stealing three shirts. It was his first offence.

58. Michael Fisher, a surprisingly well-dressed housebreaker. The 13-year-old was sentenced to four month's with hard labour for his first offence on January 1st, 1873. The first and last parts of the sentence were to be served in solitary confinement. Small boys were often used by adults to break into houses and open doors or windows from the inside.

HER MAJESTY'S HOTELS

DURHAM GAOL

Durham was one of the first prisons to experiment with the 'separate system' whereby prisoners were confined to solitary cells. The system was the result of the authorities' belief that offenders were corrupted by mixing with fellow inmates.

Previous attempts to segregate impressionable boys from hardened old lags had failed because of the inadequacies of buildings and the growing prison population. Before segregation young unconvicted prisoners on remand, with no regular cells of their own, were herded together at night in unsupervised separate dormitories where they slept in groups of between fifteen and twenty. Many spent their days in what a chaplain termed *the plague spot of the gaol*, a room where twenty to forty men and boys *from the returned transport to the innocent* mingled, without work and without supervision.

Non-remand prisoners had shared cells at night where boys regularly slept three to a bed. But conditions for the non-segregated remand prisoners were far worse, as the following descriptions, made in 1849 by two inmates, amply illustrate:

E.L. aged 42 years, for trial – acquitted – *I have been in prison for trial, partly in 'K' room, where we had no officer to look after us. The example for the boys is very bad indeed. They learn to curse and steal – and the talk at night is abominable, everything that is bad, disgusting and wicked.*

They tell tales about their robberies and about women and everything that can be said bad to corrupt the lads, this seems to be their object, and the boys listen most attentively to all that is told them. The men put the boys to fight etc.

J.B. aged 47 years, first offender – 14 days – *I sleep in a room with 14 men, seven beds, two in each bed: they talked 'sare' about all sorts of badness, how they 'sloped' their lodgings, how they carried on with bad women and how they would carry on thieving when they went out.*

They had been in all the gaols you could mention between here and London, and they talked of them, what meat they got etc...They said they would take hold of something when they got out, that they might be put in again.

Under the new regulations women were also ordered to be segregated. In the same year as the above reports, the female block was described as *the great evil.* Here as elsewhere, old lags, recidivists and young girls were grouped together in a state of near anarchy. Only one prison officer reported for duty during the day, none at night and moreover the matron, having abandoned any attempts to maintain discipline had been sacked the previous year (1848).

Following the imposition of the separate system, the increasing prison population made it impossible for all inmates to serve their punishment in solitary cells. These were allocated for a variety of reasons. Prisoners could opt for solitude, while first offenders or those considered to be a bad influence or felons who, in the governor's opinion, might benefit from the solitary experience, had little choice about serving their time in splendid isolation.

Ironically, just as Durham Prison expanded and became capable of holding more and more inmates in separate cells, prison authorities began to realise the limitations of the new system. For one thing, more and more ex-cons were re-offending after release. As early as 1863 Durham magistrates observed that *confinement in gaol under the present system had little, if any, terror to the evil-doer.*

In an article published by the *Newcastle Courant* (11.4.1879) one of the few inmates who could read and write perfectly described his admission to gaol, and life under the solitary regime.

A PRISONER'S LIFE IN NEWCASTLE GAOL

I was promptly bundled down the small flight of stairs leading from the dock, and showed into one of the cells where I found three more unfortunates, whose business had been settled by their "worships" before the case I was so deeply interested in came on...

Two of my three companions were old "gaol birds" and in high glee at what they considered a lucky arrangement of their little affair. Society was only to lose their valuable services for a period similar to my own, and they had quite made up their minds before going into the dock that through the "black list" of previous convictions against each of them they would be "fullied," by which they meant fully committed for trial at the sessions or assizes, where in all probability they would have received a much heavier punishment than the magistrates of this court are empowered to inflict...

The other prisoner owed his incarceration to conjugal infelicity; he had tinted the "optics" of his "better half," impaired her vision and general tractability and caused her successfully to seek legal redress. He paced up and down the cell like a hyena, and uttered threats of vengeance to be accomplished on his liberation. The arrival of some cold beef and bread and tea, sent by his relenting wife, however, somewhat mollified his temper, and put him in a better frame of mind. The door of our cell was again opened for the admission of three more victims – all bitten by the brewer's dog and having to undergo short periods of imprisonment owing to their disability or disinclination to pay certain fines and costs which the Bench had thought proper to impose.

59. Details of prisoners in the North-East in 1830. At this time many serious offenders were still being hanged or transported. New prisons had to be built following the colonies refusal to take any more prisoners from the motherland.

A CALENDAR of the PRISONERS

Confined in His Majesty's three Gaols of Durham, Newcastle, and Northumberland, to take their Trials, February and March, 1830 before the Honourables SIR JAMES ALLAN PARK, and SIR JAMES PARKE, Knights.

DURHAM GAOL.

JOSEPH HUTCHINSON, aged 51, charged with murder, (arraigned at the assizes held 21st February, 1829), and found not to be in a proper state of mind to take his trial.—*Still not in a proper state of mind.*

JOSEPH ORD, aged 23, charged with sheep stealing, at the assizes held 17th day of Aug., 1829.—*Acquitted.*

RALPH ATCHISON, aged 49, charged with killing and slaying James Douglas. —*28 days hard labour.*

JOS. EDWARDS, aged 23, charged with having entered the dwelling-house of Thos. English, Tudhoe, and stealing therefrom articles of wearing apparel.—*Death, recorded.*

JAMES CLARK, aged 46, charged with feloniously stealing at Houghton-le-Spring, from the person of Cuth. Harrison, 1 sov. & other monies.—*6 months imprisonment.*

MATTHEW HARRISON, aged 19, charged with having stolen from the dwelling-house of Thomas Wilkinson, at Bishop Wearmouth, 2 promissory notes, of the value of five pounds each.—*Death, recorded.*

WILLIAM PEARSON, aged 27, charged with burglariously entering the dwelling house of Misses Eliz. and Marg. Greatheads, at Darlington, with intent to commit a felony.—*No bill.*

GEORGE COULTHERD, aged 29, charged with feloniously stealing from a field, belonging to William Brown, at Parkhead, 22 sheep.—*Death.*

WILLIAM SMITH, aged 37, charged with feloniously stealing at the parish of Saint Oswald's a silk handkerchief.—*7 years transportation.*

THOS. TEESDALE, aged 30, charged with having at the parish of St. Giles, feloniously stolen a horse and cart, and a quantity of wearing apparel.—*Acquitted.*

BENJAMIN CHURCHILL, aged 27, charged with having at Sunderland, at different times put away and paid Sarah Dunn, 2 counterfeit half crowns.—*6 months.*

JOHN GRANT, aged 38, charged with feloniously stealing 2 books, the property of Fred Horn.—*6 months.*

WILLIAM DAY, aged 24, charged with having at the parish of Saint Sepulchre's, in the city of London, intermarried with Jane Coulter, his lawful wife, Ann Day, being then alive.—*7 years transportation.*

GEO. BUCKTON, aged 20, charged with stealing at Stockton, 13 bolls of wheat.—*7 years transportation.*

JANE KIRKUP, aged 26, charged with feloniously stealing from the person of Alex. Milne, a canvas bag, 17 sovs., and certain promissory notes.—*No bill.*

JANE OLIVER, aged 27, ELIZ. HOPPER, 18. charged with burglariously entering the dwelling house of Thomas Scaling, at Bishop Wearmouth, and stealing 5 notes, value £5. each, a ring, & about £5.—*Acquitted.*

FRANCIS SCOTT, aged 31, charged with having feloniously embezzled a clock.—*No bill.*

WILLIAM GATES, aged 56, ELIZ. GATES, aged 18, charged with having at Gateshead unlawfully uttered to Ann Newton, a counterfeit half-crown.—*No bill.*

MARY SPRAGGON, aged 25, charged with having at the township of Elvet, feloniously stolen from the person of Wm. Ells, the sum of £9 pounds.—*Acquitted.*

JAMES COWENS, aged 35, charged with being present, aiding, and assisting the said Mary Spraggon, to commit the felony aforesaid.

JOHN BARNETT, aged 27, charged with forging a certain instrument in writing, purporting to be a codicil to the will of the late John Marley, of Dunston Lodge, whereby the said John Barnett became possessed of the property of the said John Marley.—*Acquitted.*

THOS. THOMPSON, aged 22, charged with having feloniously stolen a mare, and a saddle and bridle, the property of John Burnip.—*Death, recorded.*

NEWCASTLE GAOL.

JOSEPH GILPATRICK, aged 23, charged with having, on the 15th day of November last, feloniously made an assault upon Edward Lawson, and stolen from him one silver watch, value £3.—*18 months impris.*

ISABELLA MILLER, aged 42, charged with having, on the 25th day of November last, feloniously stolen from James Robson, one purse, value sixpence, twenty-two sovereigns, and three half sovereigns.—*No bill.*

MARK SMITH, aged 19, and JOHN WHITFIELD BELL, aged 19, charged upon their own confession, with having, on the 2nd day of April last, feloniously broken and entered the warehouse of George Timm, and feloniously stolen 20 yards of broad cloth.

The said Mark Smith and John Whitfield Bell, also stand charged, upon their own confession, with having, on the 27th day of August last, feloniously broken the shop of Richard Young and Mark Young, and stolen 5 silver watches, 1 metal watch case, 9 gold seals, 1 watch key, 4 gold breast pins, 4 gold brooches, 2 jet brooches, and 1 silver pencil case.—*Transportation for life.*

WILLIAM BELL, aged 30, charged on a violent suspicion, with having, on the 12th day of December last, feloniously stolen from William Graham, 1 leather pocket book, and 19 promissory notes for £5. each.—*No bill.*

MATTHEW KIRKUP, aged 28, charged with having, on the 21st day of Dec. last, stolen from Wm. Anderson 3 sovs, 2 half crowns, and 5s. 2 promissory notes for £5 each, and 1 promissory note—*Transportation for life.*

CHARLES HILL, aged 14, charged on the 14th day of January last, with feloniously stealing 14 yards of black ribband, value 5s.—*7 years transportation.*

WM MANGER, aged 14, and JOHN MACPHERSON, aged 16, charged, with stealing 28 yards of rope.—*Hard labour 12 months & once privately whipped.*

RACHAEL MITCHESON, singlewoman, aged 22, charged, on the 31st day of Jan., 1829, with feloniously stealing 1 brooch, value £1.—*Acquitted.*

RICH. BEACHER, aged 21, and JANE CRAGGS, singlewoman, aged 23, charged with feloniously stealing, on the 28th day of Jan last, 1 table cloth, 2 yards of linen cloth, 1 pair of jean drawers, 1 cotton night cap, 1 sharping steel, 3 knives, 3 forks, 1 pair of scissars, and 1 book, property of Robt. Macharg ; and 1 muslin cap, and 1 cotton apron, property of Agnes Macharg.

The said Richard Beacher and Jane Craggs, also stand charged, on the same day, 2 silver tea spoons, value 5s., 1 pair of plated sugar tongs, value 6d., 2 lambs' wool stockings, value 6d, 1 pair of woman's shoes, value 1s., and 1 shoe horn, value 1d.—*Each 14 years transportation.*

ELIZ. SMITH, aged 29, and THOS. HENRY, aged 25, charged with having, on the same day, stolen 1 patched cotton counterpane, 1 cotton rug, 1 double pair of blankets, 1 linen sheet, 2 feather pillows, 2 linen pillow cases, 2 cotton pillow cases, feather bolster, 1 woollen cloth coat, 2 cotton gowns, 1 cotton apron, and 1 wobllen cloth waistcoat.—*Smith, 14 years transportation—Henry, acq.*

The said Eliz. Smith and Thos. Henry, also stand charged, on the same day, with stealing 1 chaff bolster, 1 feather pillow, 1 linen pillowslip, 1 gingham apron, 1 silk handkerchief, and 1 cotton cap, property of Joseph Atkinson.

JAMES RENOLDSON, aged 11, and JOHN RIPLEY, aged 10, charged with having, on the 8th Feb. inst. stolen 1 cow chain, value 6d, 1 iron axle, value 3d.—*9 months imprisonment and twice whipped.*

WILLIAM STEAD, aged 18, charged with stealing 2 silk handkerchiefs, value 5s.—*7 years transportation.*

JANE WILKINSON, aged 13, & MARY HUTTON, aged 11, charged with having, on the 19th Feb. inst., broken into a dwelling house, and stolen 1 bombazin gown, 1 coat, 1 waistcoat, 1 flannel petticoat, 1 cotton shift, 1 linen sheet, ½ yard of linen cloth, 1 pillow, 1 cotton shawl, 1 linen night cap, and 1 other cotton shawl.

The said Jane Wilkinson and Mary Hutton, also stand charged, with having, on the same day, burglariously broken into a dwelling-house and stolen 1 flannel shirt, 1 cotton handkerchief, and 2 towels.—*Each 14 years trans.*

MORPETH GAOL.

WILLIAM WILSON, late of Alnwick, labourer, charged with feloniously breaking and entering the dwelling-house of William Dixon, situate in the township of Warkworth, and stealing a quantity of wearing apparel, his property.—*Death, recorded.*

The same William Wilson charged with a similar of fence, at the parish of Embleton.

THOMAS QUARRY, charged with stealing a black cart horse, from Little Callerton farm, the property of Mr. Hall Raine, on the 28th of September last.

The same Thomas Quarry, charged with stealing a filly.—*Death, recorded.*

THOMAS CHURCHILL and HENRY BEAGLE, charged with breaking into a poultry-house and stealing 8 hens, his property.—*6 calender months hard labour.*

THOMAS PARKER, charged with breaking into the poultry-house of Charles Charlton, at Welton, in the parish of Ovingham, and stealing 11 ducks.—*Acquitted.*

W. Boag, Printer, Dean Street.

One of the newcomers, with an air of triumph, produced a "cutty" pipe, some tobacco, and half a dozen matches from the inside of one of his stockings – all of which contraband had escaped the inquisitive eye of the officer who searched him when taken into custody. The pipe was soon charged and lighted, and the entire company sat down upon the wooden bench, which does duty as bed, chair and table, and enjoyed the soothing weed after the fashion prevailing amongst the "red warriors of the far west." about seven o'clock our door was again thrown open, and the stentorian voice of an officer summoned us all out into the corridor, where a sergeant called over our names; we were then fettered in pairs with the handcuffs, or "snips" as they are generally called, and marched into the office of the station, where we found our escort waiting to convey us down to the prison.

With a policeman gripping each of our coat-collars, and two or three more in our wake, we received the order "Forward!" and commenced our short but undignified march down the narrow lane leading to the portals of the gaol, with a sympathising mob alongside of us, composed principally of small boys, unbonneted women and "roughs" from the odoriferous locality – the Stockbridge...

We rejoin our anonymous narrator within the prison walls:

We are next sharply ordered forward in Indian file up two or three steps, and find ourselves, after passing through another iron gate, in the "reception" room of the prison, and are handed over by the chief warder to his subordinate in charge of that department. We are then all placed in a small cell and ordered to undress. Those who can read may here make themselves acquainted with the rules of the establishment as a copy of them hangs on the wall. These are few in number and easily comprehended. Strict silence night and day is to be observed. The prisoner is not to communicate by word or sign with his fellow prisoners. He must not unnecessarily look about him either at work, at divine service, or in passing from one part of the prison to another, but is required to look straight before him. He must be industrious in the occupation provided for him, and comply promptly with the lawful orders given by those placed in authority over him. He must not barter provisions, or injure or deface any of the tools, books, bedding &c., committed to his care.

Out of this cell we are taken one by one into a well lighted room, where the warder seats himself at a desk. Each man is required to place himself in front of this officer without a particle of clothing. His personal appearance – congenital or other marks, height, age, place of birth or religion &c., are recorded. A list of his property is read over to him, his clothes are collected and placed in a net, and after the warder has satisfied himself that his charge has no prohibited articles of any description about his person, he is ushered into a closet in a corner of the room where he finds a warm bath ready for him. This he is obliged to hurriedly use, and in a half-dried state he is hustled out, presented with a bundle of prison garments, and thrust into another cell to dress.

On opening his bundle he discovers a jacket, waistcoat and trousers of a dirty whitey-brown material, something between corduroy and canvas, with a glaring yellow and white stripe on them, and the mystic monogram "N.G" (Newcastle Gaol) stencilled in various conspicuous positions. A "pork-pie" cap, shoes and stockings, shirt, under-shirt, drawers, braces and stock complete his apparel. A towel, comb, wooden spoon, and a morsel of soap are also given. As soon as each of us has undergone the inspection and bath and donned his livery, we are again formed in single file and marched across the prison yard into a rectangular building...

As soon as our party entered this building, we were each presented with a pasteboard number corresponding with the cells we were about to occupy, and this number is to be continually worn on the breast of the jacket. It fell to my lot to be confined in the south wing and here I lost sight of my companions, and was shown by a warder to my own particular lodging.

After getting me inside, he thrust in what is dignified by the title of a plank-bed – two planks about six feet by one, secured side by side with crosspieces, which give a slight elevation to one end. He pointed out my supper – a lump of dry bread – facetiously remarked that I had better quietly find out the softest portion of the planks and prepare for sleep as the gas would shortly go out, banged to the door, double-locked and bolted it, and took his departure.

When left to myself I found that I was for the time being owner of a tolerably commodious apartment about fourteen feet by ten feet, with a window of twelve panes; the furniture consisting of a rough table, stool, shelf and earth closet. A basin for ablutions and a "kit" for cleansing operations with a tap supplying cold water ad libitum, are also to be found. A bell-handle, which, when pulled rings a bell in the corridor, and causes the hinged number of the cell to start from the wall and plainly indicate to the warder where he is wanted, is provided. A tin pannikin, holding a pint, an earthenware pot for drinking purposes, together with the toilet requisites and wooden spoons served in the reception room and three large rugs, complete the not very luxurious appointments.

With the aid of those rugs and the plank-beds I managed to make a tolerably comfortable resting-place, and in the arms of Morpheus soon found a happy release from the cares and anxieties of the – to me – eventful day.

At 5.45 am three strokes of a bell announces the commencement of another working day, and if they fail to awaken any sleeper, the creaking of locks and the clanging of doors, which shortly follow will do the business. Each cell door is opened by a warder, and the occupant asked if he is "all right," and told to place outside of the door his tin pannikin, if it be required to contain any portion of his breakfast. At 6 o'clock each prisoner is supposed to be washed, dressed, have his bedding neatly folded up, and himself ready for work. At that hour a bundle or "task" of oakum, about 4lbs in weight is handed to me. This is a day's work...

The majority are still employed at oakum picking and the rest find work in mat making, ship fenders and in stone-breaking. Shoemakers and tailors respectively find employment in making and repairing the prison shoes

60. Interior of Newcastle Gaol.

and garments; blacksmiths, joiners and tinners have facilities for plying their respective crafts and all the extensive whitewashing and cleaning is effected by prison labour...

The principal punishments inflicted for ordinary breaches of discipline are forfeiture of marks, close confinement to cell, and bread-and-water diet. For repeated offences and more serious ones such as assaults on officers, window breaking &c., confinement in a dark cell on bread and water is reserved and the Governor has power to order personal chastisement if he thinks fit...

The "county crop" is no longer administered; the hair, when it requires cutting is operated upon in the ordinary way, unless its luxuriant filthiness affords a shelter to vermin when the surgeon may order a clean sweep. Shaving is abolished though some manage to perform it with the knives used at their work. Tobacco is the great want and every new comer is pestered with applications for a "bit of snout." "Snout" is "gaolic" for tobacco, and notwithstanding the strict scrutiny of the reception room, small quantities of it now and again find their way inside...

Talking between those in adjoining cells is made easy by the perforations in the walls, laboriously made by a bit of wire, which can be got from the rim of a dinner tin.

The cells are frequently visited in consequence of these offences, the holes plugged up with wood, and prompt punishments await those whose offences can be clearly brought home to them...

I can scarcely attempt to describe the feeling which possessed me, when I completed my time and found myself in my ordinary habiliments, outside the prison walls; the buoyant cheerful feeling which the Turkish bath induces is a faint approach to it. In conclusion I may say that I firmly believe that prison discipline, as it is now applied does exactly what it is intended to do. It is a severe punishment but it is also a reformatory: regular hours, plain and nutritious food, and strict temperance improve the health of the body, while the frequent religious instruction and exercises do as much for the soul, and a prisoner – if there is any good in him at all – returns to society a wiser and a better man.

MORPETH GAOL

Also known as 'the County College', 'Morpeth Hydro' and 'Her Majesty's Temperance Hotel', Morpeth Gaol provided mostly temporary accommodation for the thieves, rogues, vagabonds, prostitutes, and, above all, inebriates of the town between 1828 and 1881.

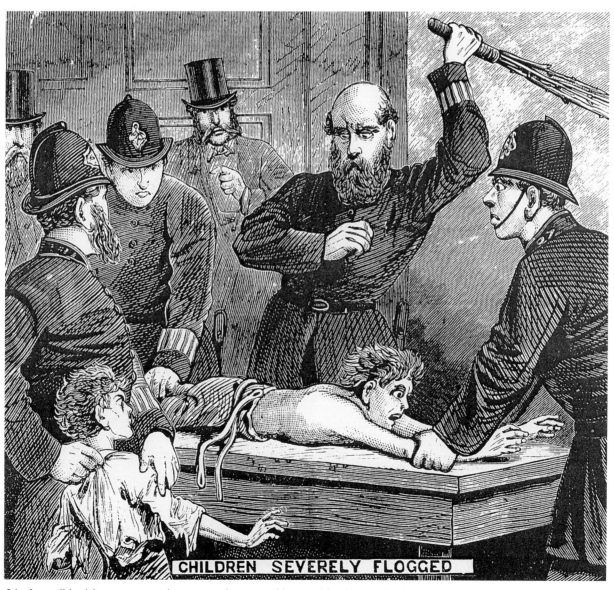

CHILDREN SEVERELY FLOGGED

61. A spell inside was sometimes supplemented by a whipping at the beginning and end of the sentence.

62. Newcastle gaol (Carliol) demolished in the 1920s.

For five inmates Morpeth was their last resting home. Three were publicly hanged in 1846 and 1847 and two privately in 1875 and 1876. All five were buried in the prison burial grounds but, like the gaol itself, their stone tombstones have long since disappeared.

In March, 1846, a 26-year-old murderer named Joicey was publicly executed for poisoning his father with arsenic. He confessed to the crime shortly before his hanging. Ralph Joicey put on a stone in weight whilst awaiting judgment day. The day of a public execution was traditionally given public holiday status. Accordingly this first such event in Morpeth since 1822 attracted a largish crowd including a reporter from the *Newcastle Advertiser:*

During the previous night snow commenced falling heavily and this it continued to do the whole morning. As early as six o'clock parties arrived from neighbouring villages and took up their position adjoining the place of execution. There they remained despite the pitiless pelting of the storm until eight o'clock.

The prison doors were thrown open, and the procession slowly emerged. The convict walked steadily and firmly yet the ashy paleness of his countenance – constitutionally ruddy – betokened the strength of his inward emotions. On coming to the outer gate, the prisoner, who had kept his eyes directed downward towards a book of devotional exercises which he held open in his hand, his hat being slouched to screen the upper portion of his face, raised his head and for a moment looked upon the scaffold at sight of which he involuntarily shuddered...The assistance of the turnkey was necessary to enable him to ascend the stairs; but when on the scaffold his eyes were closed. He took up his position under the beam without speaking a word...The cap, having been drawn over his face, and the fatal cord adjusted, the chaplain offered up a prayer.

As soon as the last amen was uttered, the bolt was drawn – the drop fell – and the murderer was launched

into eternity without a struggle. A large proportion of the crowd being employed in agricultural labour had never, perhaps, witnessed an execution before, and hence the general behaviour was better than is usually witnessed on similar occasions amongst town assemblages.

Many wept, others turned away their heads unable to bear the sickening sight. The body, after hanging the usual time, was cut down, placed in a coffin and interred within the prison walls.

A rival reporter then followed the crowd to various watering holes. Perhaps predictably his version of events was different:

A large crowd, collected from all the surrounding districts, witnessed the revolting exhibition; which, instead of proving 'a great moral lesson' was followed by drinking, singing and other excesses at the various public houses which were crammed for the rest of the day, by the sight-seers who had come to enjoy their holiday.

The authorities had problems with the indoor executions of 28-year-old Richard Charlton and 23-year-old George Hunter, it being difficult to find an area secluded from both the public and other prisoners. The architects of prisons had not foreseen the switch to private executions. Both men were eventually strung up in the South West Tower.

The gaol held an average 93 prisoners on any one day and throughout 1851, 453 prisoners served time in Morpeth. Of these 277 were English, 112 Irish and 55 Scots.

The prison was closed in 1881 and the prisoners, along with their treadmills – to make them feel at home – removed to Newcastle. The domestic utensils and surplus furnishings were sold at public auction but there was no interest in the building which was consequently demolished.

To their credit many Victorian individuals and charities sought to rescue youngsters from a life of hopelessness and crime, which seemed especially likely after a spell inside. One such northern reformer put his ideas into practice in an original manner.

James Hall was shocked and offended by the number of tear-away children on Tyneside. With the aim of turning *many of the rudest boys in all England* into worthy citizens, he founded a school on board *The Wellesley* one of the oldest sailing battleships of the line. With the help of public subscriptions, the 50-gun ship was moored off North Shields in 1868 and converted to a training ship for approximately 300 boys aged between 12 and 16.

The lads had not been convicted of any crimes but, for one reason or another, were considered at risk and likely to spend at least part of their lives at one of Her Majesty's 'hotels'.

The day began at 5 am with a cold bath. The boys were taught seamanship, swimming, diving, navigation etc with a view to their following a life on the ocean wave. Discipline was harsh, there being no holidays, and leave rarely given. The emphasis was on moral and religious training. To keep costs down the lads were responsible for making and laundering their own clothes.

Porridge was served at breakfast two mornings a week, rice with sugar and currants on another two and cocoa and bread made up the weekday morning menu.

In what was considered a treat, Sunday's breakfast was a half pint of coffee with bread.

Dinners would typically contain about 5 ozs. fresh meat, vegetables and suet pudding. Australian 'preserved' rabbit, plum pudding and reasonable allowances of bread also featured on the menu. Tea was a half-pint, served with eight ounces of bread with marmalade on Saturdays, and butter on Sundays.

By the very nature of training ship 'recruits', punishment of bread and water had to be administered periodically and some of the boys took longer than others to settle in. On the whole, however, the scheme was considered to be a success with around seventy-five per cent of the youngsters enlisting in the navy at the end of their course. The end of *The Wellesley* came when she caught fire on March 11th 1914. The absence of panic amongst the 290 lads on board testified to the discipline instilled. Clad in their blue uniforms the youngsters, many of whom were shoeless, abandoned the sinking ship by every possible means, down the accommodation ladder and via perilous descents on ropes. They were rescued by the various vessels which had assembled to render them assistance.

The following dawn saw a smouldering hulk, listing and resting on the mud-bottom of the river. It was in no way salvageable and was towed away to Jarrow slake where it lay forgotten in the mud.

The school was rehoused in Tynemouth Palace.

T.T.S. "WELLESLEY" ON FIRE, NO. SHIELDS, MAR. 11, 1914.

63. The training ship 'Wellesley' on fire off North Shields in 1914. Because of the instilled discipline not one of the boys lost their life.

64. Mary Costella, a 27-year-old prostitute, had an interesting collection of tattoos. Anthony was to be found on her left breast and Dixon on the right. Whether she had given them names or whether they were reserved for Anthony Dixon is unclear. Other tattoos included, on her right arm: an anchor, heart, M.A.E. 22 J.M. John McKie RQ.SM.SM.EHH. Anthony McLean. On her left arm she had the name Ellen Watson, her real name, perhaps? In 1872, following a long string of convictions, Mary was sent down for 15 calendar months for stealing money.

April 11th 1895. I learned at the house today that two of the inmates absconded on the 8th inst. McLaughlin and Barron. McLaughlin was the ring leader and a very bad character. They picked the lock of an outdoor. May God have mercy on them for Jesus sake.

April 16th 1895. Learned that M. Napier [an employee] was very violent and quarrelled with the inmates. Afterwards she absconded. On the 15th the curate of All Saints took her again to the house, when in his presence she made a violent attack upon an inmate. He had great difficulty in expelling her as she was under the influence of drink.

August 28th. Visited the home three times. Acting laundry woman Margaret Haddock has misconducted herself. Drunkenness – discharged.

65. Mary Ann Ross, a 34-year-old with 28 previous convictions between 1865-1873. She appeared before the court variously charged with stealing, eight times; being drunk and disorderly, eleven; for assault twice and for being a vagrant and prostitute on seven occasions. Mary Ann, a widow, was sentenced to six months in 1872. Regularly passing from one to the other, prison and oblivion were, in many ways, the only homes Mary knew.

Many charitable institutions were set up to deter young women from making their living as 'unfortunates' or prostitutes. One such establishment was the Brandling Place Home for Penitent Women. An average of eighteen girls were employed doing laundry for a large hotel. Some were encouraged to emigrate to Canada and, of the intake of 15 in 1879, eight stayed on in the home, one went to Sunderland workhouse, one left to live with her sister in Gateshead while another moved in with friends in South Shields. The penitentiary, workhouse and 'service' were the destinations for another three and just one returned to *her former evil life*.

Desperate for donations the annual reports painted a romanticised version of life in the homes. 1895 extracts from the diary of the Secretary, however, reveal that all was not sweetness and light, and indeed it appears that staff, driven to the bottle, were often as disruptive as the girls in their care:

TRIPLE EXECUTION AT DURHAM

66. Durham Gaol, the main scene of executions in the North-East.

DURHAM GAOL 2nd AUGUST, 1875

The first to rise was the Barnard Castle murderer. William McHugh (no.16) had slept soundly and appearing cheerful was up and dressed by 5.15 am. He'd adapted well to prison life and even relished the supplemented diet, which included a daily ration of beer, that was the fare of anyone in the death cell. On this particular morning breakfast consisted of tea and bread and half a pound of beefsteak. McHugh nibbled a few crumbs and sipped at his tea: his appetite had finally failed him. Abandoning his last meal he entered into fervent prayer with the priest.

Gilligan (no.7) slept until 6 am. Woken by the warder in charge, he was proffered the same fare as McHugh. But the Darlington murderer also preferred to make his peace with God.

The third prisoner, Pearson (no.14), also spent a good night. With no appetite at all, she merely gulped down a few sips of tea as she listened intently to the gaol chaplain endeavouring to prepare her for the afterlife.

Michael Gilligan, who occupied the regular condemned cell, was the first to be summoned by the hangman. Led into the No.2 classroom, he was met by Marwood, who stealthily and silently adjusted the condemned man's body strap. McHugh was then brought in. The two felon's wild eyes met for a few seconds. All colour drained from Gilligan's face. Silence followed.

Marwood then marched to the chaplain's room in the female wing to summon the third person to the summer morning's grisly proceedings.

The slow walk to the scaffold commenced.

The Under-Sheriff, the Deputy-Governor and Chief Warder Smith were followed placidly by McHugh, the Reverend William Rooney and the senior warders. Behind came Gilligan and Canon Committ with the other warders. All journalists were denied entry.

Leaving the schoolroom the pitiful procession passed through to the female wing and, turning at a sharp angle, were immediately confronted by a triangle of dangling nooses. Here they were met by Elizabeth Pearson, who had approached by another corridor. The two men walked with a firm step and without assistance to the gallows.

McHugh was the first to be placed under the second beam and to have the fatal rope adjusted. He hardly changed colour. Not so Gilligan, who came next. His face was deathly pale.

The woman, Pearson, though paying earnest attention to her spiritual adviser, was an eye-witness to the positioning of the two men, whose legs Marwood now pinioned. She, herself, was then placed under the first beam, immediately in front of the two men with her back to them. Having walked to the scaffold without assistance, Pearson remained, throughout the proceedings, the most self-possessed of the three.

The condemned souls were now earnestly speaking to God in subdued but audible voices. One can only wonder as to what passed through the minds of those who prayed for mercy though they themselves showed none. All three were murderers.

Some five months previously 28-year-old Elizabeth Pearson had coldbloodedly poisoned her uncle in Gainford. Elizabeth had volunteered to keep house for James Watson following the death of his wife, but the younger woman had very peculiar ideas about geriatric care. Once ensconced in the kitchen, Elizabeth added the best part of two packets of Beatties' Vermin Powder to the old man's regular medicine. James immediately complained of stomach pains and was then seized by a fit of trembling. Wracked in agony, he threw his head back and clenched his hands, before collapsing to the floor. He died like a poisoned rat.

Elizabeth spent little time in divesting body of clothes and house of furnishings, but this haste proved her undoing. The victim's son, Robert, smelt a rat and a post mortem was subsequently ordered. The analysis of the stomach contents revealed the presence of large quantities of strychnine and Prussian Blue, a nasty mix of iron and cyanide.

In court defence argued that there was a lack of motive and that a 'virgin powder' had been administered by a mystery lodger, named Smith, who had conveniently since departed. Found guilty after sixty minutes of deliberation, there was no recommendation of mercy for Pearson the pensioner poisoner. Her last desperate bid to save her skin, on the grounds that she was pregnant, failed following examination by the prison surgeon. When news of this failure was broken to her husband and son, both male members of the family were seen to be weeping bitterly as they left the prison gates. This was to be their final meeting with the woman they both loved.

At 36, William McHugh was the eldest participant of the Durham triple hanging. His crime, like so many others then as now, was executed whilst under the influence, a fate, he too, would doubtless have preferred. In fact, it was McHugh's partiality to a drop that brought about his downfall. On the evening of April 11th an argument over a bottle of whiskey had flared up in Barnard Castle. The row involved McHugh, his friend William Gallager and a man named Thomas Mooney and resulted in Mooney being pushed over a wall, into the river. In a bizarre legal decision McHugh and Gallager were jointly tried for murder. On the balance of evidence the jury decided that Gallager, thinking better of it, had had no part in pushing Mooney into the river. Accordingly the latter was acquitted, but the unfortunate McHugh was condemned to death.

For his part, 22-year-old Michael Gilligan made no effort to deny his role in a gang murder. He did, however, vehemently protest that the only reason he was being sent to the gallows was because of his nationality: Gilligan was Irish.

The facts of the case seem to prove Gilligan's point. On Easter Sunday 1875, Gilligan and six accomplices scoured the pubs of Darlington in search of a man named Kilcran, whom the gang accused of crossing them. When found he was mercilessly beaten and later died from his injuries. Within a very short time, three of Kilcran's seven assailants were apprehended, but the others escaped. Of the three arrested, two were sentenced to fifteen years for manslaughter, but Gilligan, perhaps due to anti-Fenian feeling prevalent in the country, was sentenced to hang. A large petition was organised by Gilligan's sympathisers in Darlington but to no avail.

The fates of the Durham three were sealed on the Saturday prior to their execution, when the following missive was received from the Home Office:

"Sir – in reply to your letter of the 10th inst I am directed by Mr Secretary Cross to acquaint you that he does not propose advising any interference with the course of law in the case of Michael Gilligan, Elizabeth Pearson and William McHugh now under sentence of death in Durham prison for wilful murder.
I am yours obediently, A.F.O. Liddell."

There was no more time for reflection. No time for regrets. On a warm summer's morning while the citizens of Durham set about their humdrum chores, two men and one woman mumbled their final prayers.

Marwood then gave the signal.

The three ministers shook hands with their charges and had barely left the trapdoor before the hangman pulled the lever. The three dropped with a heavy thud at exactly three minutes past eight.

Death was almost instantaneous. Gilligan, the heaviest of the three, struggled slightly but there were no violent contortions as the victims had each fallen some six feet. Marwood's methods were a vast improvement on those of his predecessor, Calcraft, who habitually allowed a drop of two and a half feet.

After the deaths of Marwood's latest clients, the black flag was raised above Durham Prison. The bodies were put into coffins after hanging the customary hour. McHugh, a father of five, and Gilligan (one), were buried in a long line of male murderers. Mrs. Pearson was interred to the right of the grave of a fellow-poisoner, Mary Ann Cotton.

DURHAM SUMMER ASSIZES IN 1875

No.	Name	Age	Trade	Offence as charged	Verdict	Sentence
1	Andrew Donaldson	28	Boilermaker	Burglariously breaking and entering the dwelling-house of William Bell, and stealing therein four pounds in money, and a Swedish coin, the property of the said William Bell and Joseph Bell, at Bishopwearmouth, 15th August, 1874	Guilty	12 cal. months hard labour
2	Richard Warne	25	Pitman	Feloniously wounding Arthur Samuel Dow, with intent to do grievous bodily harm, at Chester-le-Street, 27.2.1875.	Guilty	7 years penal servitude
3	John Pearson	45	Labourer	Bigamy by marrying Matilda Rollings, Jane Rosanna, his former wife, being then alive, at Newcastle-upon-Tyne, 21st October 1866.	Pleaded guilty	12 cal. months hard labour
4	John Tully	42	Labourer	Wilful murder of Bridget Tully, at Throston, 24th March,1875. NO BILL	Guilty of assault	9. cal. months hard labour
5	Matthew Oliphant	18	Goods Guard	Carnally knowing and abusing Elizabeth Harrison, a girl under the age of ten years, to wit, of the age of seven years at Gateshead, 28.3.1875. NO BILL	Guilty of an indecent assault	15 cal. months hard labour
6	Joseph Cooper	14	Whitesmith	Forging an order for the delivery of four hundred weight of lead, with intent to defraud James Kindler, at Stockton. 12th February, 1875.	Pleaded guilty	12 cal. months hard labour
7	Michael Gilligan	22	Labourer	Wilful murder of John Kilcran, at Darlington, 28th March, 1875	Guilty of murder	To be hanged
8	James Durkin	33	Labourer	Aiding and abetting Michael Gilligan to murder John Kilcran, at Darlington 28th March 1875. Charged on indictment with No 7 for murder.	Both Guilty of manslaughter	15 years penal servitude each
9	James Flinn	21	Striker			
10	Robert McKenzie	45	Striker	Manslaughter of Mary Ann Law at Stockton, 9th April, 1875.	Not guilty	Discharged
11	Michael Ferguson	17	Pitman	Rape on Elizabeth Jane Vaughan at Trimdon, 11th April, 1875.	....	Discharged
12	Samuel Arms	...	....	*Arms admitted to bail.* NO BILL		
13	John McDermott	38	Pitman	Feloniously wounding Philip Turnbull with intent to do grievous bodily harm at Durham, 27th March, 1875	Guilty of unlawfully wounding	18 cal. months hard labour
14	Elizabeth Pearson	28	Married	Wilful murder of James Watson at Gainford, 15th March, 1875	Guilty of murder	To be hanged
15	James Ditchburn	22	Pitman	Robbery of Joseph Lake with violence, at Bishop Auckland, 30th March, 1875	Guilty	5 years penal servitude
16	William McHugh	36	Hawker	Wilful murder of Thomas Mooney, at Barnard Castle, 11th April, 1875	Guilty of murder	To be hanged
17	William Gallager	35	Labourer		Not guilty of murder	Discharged
18	Henry Stoker	32	Pitman	Robbery of Forster Minto with violence at Chester-le-Street, 3rd May, 1875	Both not guilty	Both discharged
19	Stephen Ramshaw	31	Pitman			

No.	Name	Age	Trade	Offence as charged	Verdict	Sentence
20	George Plummer	21	Pitman	Wilful murder of Sarah Forster, at Brandon 26th April, 1875	Not guilty on the ground of insanity	To be detained during Her Majesty's pleasure.
21	Thomas Dublin	42	Labourer	Feloniously wounding Richard Parkinson, with intent to murder at Stockton, 25th April, 1875	Guilty of wounding with intent to do GBH	7 years penal servitude
22	William Nevins	19	Pitman	Robbery of Robert Hardman with violence at Winlaton, 24th April, 1875	Both not guilty	Both discharged
23	John McLean	23	Soldier			
24	Thomas McKenna	20	Labourer	Feloniously wounding Alexander Conway with intent to do grievous bodily harm, at Jarrow, 4th May, 1875	Both guilty	6 cal. months hard labour
25	John Cassidy	23	Labourer			9 cal. months hard labour
26	Ralph Errington	28	Pitman	Feloniously wounding Thomas Stevenson with intent to do grievous bodily harm, at Haswell 9th May, 1875	Both guilty	5 years penal servitude each
27	Thomas Brown	48	Pitman			

Multiple hangings were far from typical but the Durham Assizes was having a far from typical summer. The accompanying chart shows just how busy they were. Richard Warne (no.2) was seriously behind with his rent. After a showdown he begrudgingly handed over 26 shillings to his landlord, Samuel Dow. Warne insisted that he be given a receipt, which was duly furnished. The lodger, who was illiterate, professed himself to be dissatisfied with Dow's *queer writing* and insisted a stamp should be placed upon his receipt. The landlord refused to comply with this request and, after an afternoon spent drinking, brooding, moping and feeling sorry for himself, an increasingly irate Warne returned to his lodgings and mounted a murderous assault upon Dow, battering the hapless landlord with a pickhandle. The judge was minded to pass a very harsh sentence on Warne, as a deterrent to others.

John Tully (no.4), whose case is mentioned in Chapter 4, was initially accused of murdering his wife Bridget. The post-mortem determined that she had died of natural causes.

(No 5). Matthew Oliphant's young victim was the daughter of his Gateshead landlady. In her mother's absence Oliphant assaulted the child as he was putting her to bed, after first threatening her with a severe thrashing if she 'told'. The hideous offence was compounded when the poor girl was later found to be suffering from an *odious disease* passed on by her assailant.

Prisoner Joseph Cooper, (no.6) stopped being a free man and became a number after the judge sent him down. The young whitesmith was one of the few people to be praised by the beak on sentencing, albeit *for exercising a great deal of cunning.*

Robert McKenzie (no.10) was a striker in more ways than one. On April 1st he struck his partner Mary Ann Law about the head with a saucer when she refused to give him money for drink. Erysipelas set in to a severe wound on the side of her head and Mary died as the result of her ill-treatment. McKenzie's defence was that his partner had fallen down the stairs whilst drunk. The jury returned a verdict of not guilty on the grounds of insufficient evidence

John McDermott (no.13) fancied himself as a hard man and boasted in the Junction Inn at Gilersgate that he did not care for any man in Durham. He went on to call Philip Turnbull's wife a prostitute and was duly pursued into the road by an outraged husband. The ensuing brawl resulted in Turnbull being confined to bed with stab wounds for fourteen days. When apprehended later that evening, McDermott, with the brashness of the drunk, admitted his guilt: *I did it. What of it?* The following morning, with the wariness of sobriety, Turnbull changed his story, insisting: *I know nothing of it.* Because this was his first offence the sentence was less than McDermott must have been anticipating, for on hearing it he bucked the trend of insulting the beak with a polite, *Thankee, Sir.*

James Ditchburn (no 15) was the unlucky one of three robbers. He was caught. The trio approached Joseph Lake and spun him a sob story about loosing all their money at Durham races. Joseph, a miner who lived at Eldon, stood three quarts of ale in compensation. The impecunious gamblers repaid his generosity by attacking him outside the pub and stealing £1/11/6d of his hard earned wage. During the course of the assault, one of Lake's assailants lay across his face so he could not raise the alarm, while another bit his finger. Ditchburn's sentence was harsh as he had three previous convictions.

67. Most assault cases coming before the court were between drunken men. Many were attacked after leaving public houses where they had inadvertently shown their wealth.

(No 17), William Gallager, was one of the luckiest men ever to walk free from court. His fellow accused, William McHugh, would dangle at the end of a rope less than two months later. After sentencing McHugh to hang, the judge addressed his 'innocent' accomplice. Mr Justice Archibald appears to have been in no doubt that a miscarriage of justice had been perpetrated in his court:

As for you Gallager, the jury has acquitted you of this offence, and you must be discharged and I can only say that your conduct throughout the whole of this transaction will merit the execration, contempt and indignation of every right-minded person. You are now discharged.

Pitmen Stoker and Ramshaw (18 and 19) gambled away most of their weekly wages at the Swan Public House. The man who pocketed the spoils, Forster Minto, was subsequently attacked from behind and robbed shortly after leaving the pub. Charged with this assault, the case against the two miners was dismissed in the absence of positive proof of identity. Minto had been very drunk and challenging people to fights all evening. The missing money, defence argued, had probably dropped out of his pocket during the course of an earlier skirmish. Had the jury known, however, that both Stoker and Ramshaw had convictions for similar offences, they may well have returned a different verdict

(No 21), Thomas Dublin, defended himself in court. During the course of a game of cards in the yard of the Shoulder of Mutton in Stockton, Dublin accused a fellow-lodger, Richard Parkinson, of being a bully. It was a clear case of the pot calling the kettle. Dublin then fell

A PASSIVE RESISTER.

68. Few offenders came quietly and policemen ran the serious risk of being attacked by friends of those arrested.

upon Parkinson. During the ferocious fight that ensued the alleged bully was stabbed in the side and some seven inches of his intestines slid through the wound. The shock of the injury almost caused Parkinson's death and his life was on the line for seventeen days. When apprehended, Dublin showed no remorse for his actions and alleged that his victim was one of a gang of Fenians. He added that he was quite willing to shoot them all as soon as the Government gave the word.

Nevins and McLean (22 and 23), charged with violently robbing one Robert Hardman, were acquitted because of lack of evidence against them. For some unknown reason it was fairly common for Victorian drunkards to openly count their money before leaving the pub. At 11pm on the night of 24th April, Robert Hardman totted up some £2/8/- shortly before staggering out of Rowland Gill's public house in Winlaton. He'd had a good evening, spending over seven shillings on beer for himself and some new found friends. Some of these 'friends' then followed him, knocked him unconscious and dumped him in an outhouse, minus his purse.

Cassidy and McKenna (24 and 25) stepped over the boundaries of the simple pub brawl when they took offence to Alexander Conway's nose and bit it. The offence, which occurred in Richardson and Ray's Public House, might have been forgiven and forgotten had the two men not then pursued their victim to the railway station and treated him to a thorough thrashing.

The assault by Errington and Brown (26 and 27) was even more serious, this being reflected in their sentences. The two poachers were caught netting rabbits and ordered off by a gamekeeper at 4 am. They replied to the command by throwing stones and hurling insults. Noticing that the keeper was alone, they crept up behind him and hit him over the head with an iron bar. A fierce struggle ensued during which the gamekeeper produced a gun. The firearm was taken from him and following a ferocious assault with both fists and boot he was left unconscious. So badly hurt was Thomas Stevenson, that the only way he could eventually raise the alarm was by crawling to the police station on his hands and knees.

Of great interest, both to court reporters and their readers, was the trial of William Plummer (no. 20), who was arraigned for the apparently motiveless shooting of one of the few people who brought pleasure to his life, his bride-to-be, Sarah Forster. Just prior to the murder the young man had been fascinated by an illustration in the *London Clipper* which showed a man slashing his sweetheart's throat and then killing himself. He was so fond of the illustration that he tore it out of the journal and went round proudly showed it to everyone he met. During the trial it was noted by the *Durham Chronicle* that *a great number of ladies were present.* This was not uncommon but less usual was the fact that the same paper then listed the entire jury, both by name and profession. Plummer was tried by a wholesale grocer, a coalfitter, a colliery agent, a viewer, a shipbroker, a shipowner, a builder, a hosier, two farmers and two butchers.

Plummer's defence admitted their client had twice shot his victim. The second bullet – being discharged about sixty seconds after the first – ruled out all pleas of either manslaughter or accidental death. In light of this, and of the prisoner's lack of cooperation, the defending lawyers sought to convince the jury that Plummer was insane and therefore not responsible for his actions.

Throughout the trial, reported in great detail, the skinny, gaunt, former collier sat crouched with his head

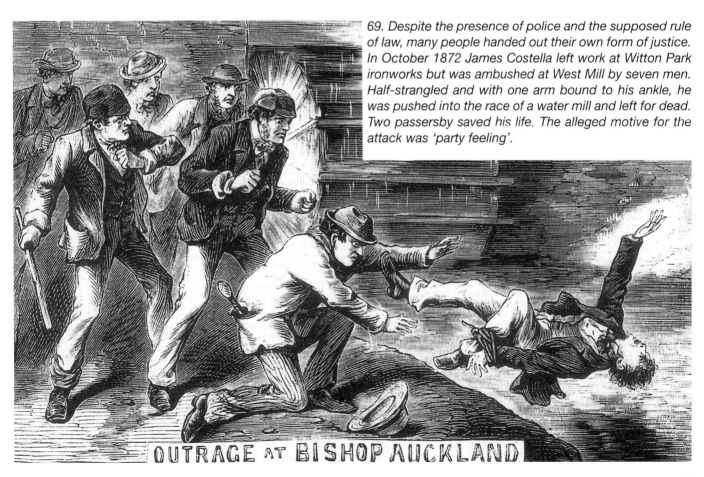

69. Despite the presence of police and the supposed rule of law, many people handed out their own form of justice. In October 1872 James Costella left work at Witton Park ironworks but was ambushed at West Mill by seven men. Half-strangled and with one arm bound to his ankle, he was pushed into the race of a water mill and left for dead. Two passersby saved his life. The alleged motive for the attack was 'party feeling'.

OUTRAGE AT BISHOP AUCKLAND

70. William Plummer in an apparently motiveless attack shot his bride-to-be at Brandon in 1875.

between his knees. The defendant's mother was the first to take the stand and testified movingly in a bid to save her son from the gallows. Let's listen to the proceedings:

DURHAM CROWN COURT Friday July 9th 1875

Mary Elizabeth Harding (mother – remarried 14 years previously).

As a boy he was always fond of fire-arms, ever since he was eight or nine years old. When he was a little child he had small cannons and pistols. After he dropped his amusements generally fire-arms were the only things he took a delight in. When about 16, unknown to me, he bought a six-barrelled revolver at Bristol. He afterwards exchanged that with Mr Pape of Newcastle for another, and since he bought another revolver. He also bought a pistol of Mr Teesdale at Durham, and a small Derringer when he lived at Chester Moor. He had also a dagger-knife. When he went out he had always some of these fire-arms with him...

My son for the last three years has been weakly and delicate, particularly when he was growing fast. Between 17 and 18 he grew five inches in a year. He was very languid and weary sick at times and off his appetite – cold feet and hands...He used to be cheerful until lately...For the last year particularly I have noticed him to be at a loss

for words when speaking. When he was talking he could not remember what he wanted to speak about. In the middle of a sentence he was at a loss for words and could not remember names and places.

He was in the habit of sitting about in his room and not talking to anybody. At other times he would be very restless and wander about. He rested very badly at nights and that increased the last six months. In consequence I had frequently to get up and go into his room. I was obliged to get him something to take and wrap his feet in warm flannels. He had no heat and was as if he had no blood in him...I have heard him say on various occasions that he would not care if he was dead...latterly he was cheerful in the presence of the poor girl Sarah Foster, but quite miserable after she was gone.

At the time they came in I was the only person in the house. I heard them talking and not in an angry tone at all. When I heard them come in at the front door I turned round to go and meet them. I was first coming towards the door when I heard the report of fire-arms. Immediately after hearing the report I saw the deceased falling over. The prisoner was at that time about two yards from her. I saw something like fire-arms in his hand, but I could not see what it was. I believe it was in his right hand. I saw the smoke. When I saw that I dropped and fainted on the floor. When I recovered consciousness I found deceased lying on the floor quite dead. The deceased was bleeding from her mouth. My son had then left the house. I then went to the back-door and saw my husband coming. I again sunk back in a fainting condition until he came in.

Mary Hudson

I am the wife of Thomas Hudson and live at No. 8, Queen-street, Brandon Colliery. About half-past four o'clock on the 26th April, I went into Harding's house and found the deceased on the floor, bleeding from wounds. The same evening I washed the deceased and saw three wounds – one on the neck, one on the back and another on the chest.

P.C. John Kirkup:

I am stationed at Brandon. On Monday, the 26th, I went to Harding's house. I saw the deceased lying in the front room. She was laid on her back with her feet pointing to the fire. She was bleeding from the mouth. There was a quantity of blood under her head and neck on the left eye. I went for Mr Nairn, Dr. Stewart's assistant but he was not at home. I afterwards searched for the prisoner, and next morning between four and five o'clock I searched all the privies and outhouses in Queen-street. On Tuesday night I went to a privy in Princess-street, and on pushing open the door I found the prisoner inside. I handcuffed him, and then Sergt. Cowen came up.

Sergt John Cowen.

I was present when P.C. Kirkup apprehended the prisoner. I searched him and found two five-chambered revolvers. Every barrel was loaded. I brought him to the station and charged him with the wilful murder of Sarah Foster. He replied 'Yes, very well'. I searched him again and found a watch and gold chain and £5.14.4, in gold, silver and copper, two pistol caps and a handkerchief, which he was wearing round his neck when apprehended.

There then followed hour after hour of medical questions and answers as to whether the young man knew what he was doing. The defence argued that there was no motive for the crime. The acts of shooting his sweetheart in the mouth one minute after first shooting her in the back and of then secreting the gun under a sofa, were not the actions of a bad man but of a mad one, it was argued.

The Crown replied that they did not have to prove motive and went on to ridicule one of the defence's arguments in favour of insanity, namely that Plummer did not know the year of his birth. The prosecuting attorney speculated as to how many pitmen in the county of Durham would have to be sent to an asylum if the telling of the year of their birth were to be regarded as a test of sanity.

In a very fair summation the judge slated the *London Clipper* and other *miserable papers* for contributing to the young girl's death. After seventy minutes the jury returned and the wholesale grocer stood to give their verdict:

Not guilty, on the grounds of insanity.

After a considerable pause his Lordship curtly addressed the prisoner:

I order you to be detained during her Majesty's pleasure.

Plummer left the court without comment, but on this occasion he did not need the assistance of the warders.

CLEVER CAPTURE OF A THIEF AT AUCKLAND.

71. A scene from 1877. Most thefts were opportunistic and only the rich lived in fear of burglars. The poor could leave their doors unlocked as they had very little worth stealing.

BRITAIN'S WICKEDEST WOMAN

**MARY ANN COTTON –
DEAD BUT NOT FORGOTTEN**

*72. The only known photograph of Mary Ann Cotton,
taken in the early 1870s by a police photographer.*

Cases of women poisoning various members of their families were rare, though not entirely unheard of; wholesale poisoning, on the other hand, is virtually unique in the annals of British crime.

Mary Ann Cotton would certainly be in the running for the title of Britain's most wicked woman. She showed her husbands, paramours and children the kind of love usually associated with black widow spiders. Anyone who stood in the way of her pursuit of 'happiness' met a swift and agonising death. Wherever she went she left in her wake a long trail of corpses, almost certainly more than twenty, five of whom were her own children. Against all the laws of probability they were all victims of gastric fever, or so Mrs Cotton asserted, before her luck ran out.

The shocking details of her crimes featured in newspapers throughout the country and from the start of her 1873 trial at Durham Court, the courtroom was packed to overflowing with outraged spectators desperate for every sordid feature of the activities of this affront to Victorian womanhood.

As opposed to the femme fatale they'd heard about,

what they saw on the opening day of the trial was a haggard female, very down in the mouth, aged somewhere between 34 and 40. Standing with her head bowed, Mary Ann Cotton. was charged with four counts of murder. The specimen victims were Charles Edward Cotton (the defendant's stepson), who died on July 12th 1872; her lodger-lover Joseph Nattrass (April 1st 1872); another stepson, Frederick Cotton (March 10th 1872) and Robert Cotton, Mary's natural son, who departed this life on March 29th of the same year.

The first case brought by the prosecution was the most recent death, that of Charles Edward Cotton, the prisoner's 7-year-old stepson. Outlining its case the Crown quickly skipped over Mary's early life, pointing out that she had been employed as a nurse at Sunderland Infirmary and married four times. She and her last husband, Frederick Cotton, a collier, took up residence in West Auckland in 1871 and he died of gastric fever a short time later. It was at this point that the prosecution went into more detail about the murders and because of this stratagem the jury never learnt about Mary's earlier history, which makes for chilling reading even now. We, however, are not so constrained.

Said to have been born at East Rainton in 1833, Mary was a regular worshipper in the chapel where she later taught Sunday School. At the age of 14, and said to be the prettiest child in the village, Mary was not short of male admirers. Following a brief spell as a domestic servant she married a sailor named Mowbray. The family moved to the south coast where all four of their children subsequently died from gastric fever. While on home leave shortly after the death of his last child Mr Mowbray ate his last home-cooked meal and died of the same disease. Throughout her life Mary was most insistent that only she would cook and 'care' for her husbands/lovers and children. Yet gastric fever dogged her every culinary step, even taking out her sister-in-law and her two children.

Mary was a truly fatal attraction. Moving to Seaview she teamed up with a man named Nattrass but, as he was already married, she subsequently turned her attentions onto one of her rich hospital patients. George Wade bequeathed everything he owned to his *beautiful 25-year-old wife* before succumbing to Mary Ann Cotton syndrome.

Not the type of person to stay in mourning for long, Mary moved in with a foreman, James Robinson, and his four motherless children. In the due course of time she produced another child before yet another outbreak of gastric fever saw all five of them bedded in the cemetery. Mr Robinson was spared the family illness, probably because he had the good fortune to discover his wife helping herself to his savings. He gave her the key to the street.

Following a brief spell as a matron in Sunderland Penitentiary our heroine moved in with a sea-captain and promptly stole his worldly goods whilst he was at sea. In search of more to spend she then fleeced one Dr. Heffern of Spennymoor. Following the sudden and unexpected death by gastric fever of her fourth husband, Frank Cotton, Mary returned to her former lover, Joseph Nattrass, whose wife had recently died. He too would eventually succumb to the ubiquitous gastric fever.

Back in the courtroom, Mr Russell, acting for the prosecution, focused the jury's attention on the alleged murder of the child, Charles Edward Cotton. One of the witnesses was Sarah Smith, wife of William Smith, pitman, West Auckland:

I have known the prisoner since she came to West Auckland. Her name then was Mary Ann Cotton. She lived a few doors from me; and her husband, Frederick Cotton, lived in the house with her, and also two children by his former wife, and one by the prisoner. The name of her own child was Robert Robson Cotton; and the other two children were called Frederick and Charles Edward. Charles Edward was about 7 years old, Frederick about 10 years old, and Robert a few months old. Her husband Frederick Cotton, died about three months after the family came to Auckland. The boy Frederick Cotton died early in 1872. Robert Robson Cotton also died early in 1872. I remember a lodger named Nattrass who lived in prisoner's house. He did not live in the house in July when Charles Edward Cotton died. Nattrass died on Easter Monday (April 1st). I remember Charles Edward Cotton dying on a Friday in July.

The next door neighbour, Mary Ann Dodds, a cleaner in Cotton's house, remembered Charles affectionately:

...he was a particularly fine little boy for going errands, or anything of that kind. He was active and healthy when I saw him last alive. I saw him on the night of Saturday, July 6th.

Just six days later the neighbour was cleaning his corpse:

I was sent for about twenty minutes past six o' clock on Friday morning. The prisoner told me the child had died about ten minutes to six that morning. I washed the body and laid it out. When I arrived the body was upon a sofa upstairs. The prisoner said that as far as she could think the child had died of gastric fever.

Mary Dodds later told the court that six weeks previously she had been sent by the defendant to the chemist to buy soft soap and arsenic to rub on the iron bedstead to kill bed bugs. The remaining preparation, containing at least 240 grains of arsenic, was subsequently stored in a jug. Three grains was sufficient to kill any child.

Many witnesses testified as to the cruelty shown by the Cotton children's wicked step-mother. Mary Tate, who washed and cleaned for the Cottons, told the court:

On Easter Sunday I went to prisoner's house, and the little boy was crying for an egg and an orange that Mrs Smith had given him. Prisoner took the orange out of her pocket and tossed it on to the fire, she said the boy should not have it. She whipped the boy very much with a leather strap.

When questioned as to whether she beat her own children Mary Tate replied:

I have a boy and he cries sometimes and I whip him at times; but there is no reason in whipping children. The prisoner used the flat of her hand in striking the boy on the face and head and different parts...I have never whipped my boy as the prisoner whipped her boy. The strap was a strap which a pitman generally wears round his waist when at work. The strap had a buckle.

Mary Ann Cotton's penchant for cruelty was corroborated by a pitman, William Davidson:

I saw the prisoner beating him on Saturday before he died. She was beating him with a doubled belt, and it looked to be leather. She beat him a canny bit, and then gave over. She beat him a good deal. She stopped and began again.

Another witness also saw the thrashing which ended with Cotton dashing the boy's head against the door-post.

This particular attack followed a refusal by the workhouse to take in the unwanted stepson unless Mary Ann Cotton accompanied him. An earlier attempt to procure lodgings for the seven-year-old, with a relation in Ipswich, had also failed. To workhouse officials Cotton had argued that it was a great hardship for her to be taxed with the boy when she had the opportunity of taking in a respectable lodger. Having heard of Mary Cotton's association with yet another man, Thomas Riley, the assistant-overseer at the workhouse, asked: *I suppose you are going to be married to Mr Mann?* Cotton had simply replied: *It may be so.*

Despite her overt brutality, it was an unguarded, off-hand remark during the course of the above conversation that led Cotton into the dock. Cotton speculated that perhaps she would not be troubled long by her unwanted stepson, as the boy was sure to go the way of the rest of his family. Looking the healthy boy up and down, Riley was astonished at this comment. He put his hand on the boy's head and asked: *You don't mean to tell me that this fine little fellow is going to die?* He received the ambiguous reply: *He won't get up*, which the workhouse overseer took to mean that the child would not reach adulthood. Charles Edward Cotton's fate was sealed at that point, but so was his step-mother's. Upon hearing of the child's death, just one week later, Mr Riley promptly went to the police and informed them of his suspicions.

A post-mortem was carried out and notes made of the extent of external injuries on the youngster's body but the examination was so rushed that vital evidence was overlooked with the result that the coroner's jury returned a verdict of death from natural causes. On the face of it, Mary Ann Cotton appeared to have got away with murder once again.

Curiously, however, the pathologist took part of the deceased child's stomach, small intestines and liver home where he quietly buried them in his garden. Subsequently, following the inquest, and with a little more time on his hands, the medical man re-examined the contents of Charles Edward's organs and found them to contain arsenic. Over the next few months four bodies were exhumed and all deaths were deemed to have been caused by arsenical poisoning. The children had been given small but fatal doses of the poison, but Nattrass had been given enough to kill him more than five times over.

At the trial, her defence did not dispute the cause of death but argued that the poison may have been introduced accidentally. They were certainly clutching at straws by suggesting that such vast amounts of the arsenic may have come from the wallpaper.

In its summation the Crown left few in doubt as to the verdict the jury would return. Mary Ann Cotton had the means (the left-over arsenic), the motive (she wanted to once again start a new life) and the opportunity to end her young charge's life. The reports state:

…on July 6, 1872 the once numerous household had dwindled down and consisted only of the prisoner, and the boy Charles Edward Cotton, into whose death they were inquiring and this had an importance in this case that was overwhelming in its character.

No servant in the house, no lodger in the house, no inmate of any kind in the house. This child of seven years of age, face to face with a woman not his mother, who had shown no signs of motherly tenderness (to put it at the least) in her heart towards him; and he was a tie she would readily have got rid of – he was a tie irksome to her, and a tie she tried to get rid of but failed. The boy had been described by a witness as a rather pale lad, but a fine active healthy little fellow; and even the joyless character of his life, which seemed never to have been warmed by the sunshine of a mother's love, could not entirely stamp out that spontaneous joyness which nature implanted in him. On July 6th he was seen well, active, healthy...on the very day she complained that the boy could not be taken into the workhouse...this healthy child took ill; and before seven days had passed the child had died, – faded away not slowly, but collapsed quickly and was hurried into a grave in a week.

The defence had an almost impossible job summing up but Mary Ann Cotton wept bitterly as she listened to her advocate, Mr Foster, fighting vainly for her life. His main argument centred around there being no motive for murdering Nattrass. He also argued that no mother could be as wicked as to take the life of her 14-month-old baby:

One almost revolted at such a picture – a mother poisoning her own child – a mother watching her own child, nursing it, calling in the doctor, dancing it upon her knee, listening to its prattle, watching its smile, while she knew she had been administering doses of arsenic, and watching its limbs writhing, as it smiled in her face, and hoped for support and protection. Depend on it a mother could do nothing of the kind.

So well did the defence attorney speak, with all the evidence stacked against him, that scattered applause broke out in areas of the court and had to be quickly stifled by the judge.

The jury deliberated fifty minutes before returning a 'guilty' verdict. The blood drained from the heavily pregnant Mary Ann Cotton's face and she seemed on the point of collapse when asked if she had anything to say. She replied in a scarcely audible whisper, *Not guilty*. Following the sentence of death the convicted murderess had to be helped from court by the matron and attendant wardresses.

Cotton's stepfather visited her three days before her execution, he wanted to discover the truth about the accusations and to tell her that her *wicked habits* had shortened her stepmother's days: *Now, Mary Ann, thou has not long to live and if thou has anything to confess do so now.* Mary Ann Cotton was defiant to the last and her first admission to her stepfather must be one of the understatements of nineteenth century criminal history. She thought she was probably responsible for the child's death but it had not been intentional:

Father, I have not led a good life but I am innocent of the crimes laid to my charge. I know the public are against me but I am going to die for a crime I am as innocent of as the child unborn.

On the morning of her execution Cotton breakfasted on a few sips of tea. Throughout her time in prison she had refused religious counsel but during her last few hours was most devout and contrite. She prayed with the three wardresses who'd attended her day and night in the death cell and, recalling her childhood Sunday school lessons, declared her favourite hymn to be 'Rock of Ages'.

Because of her violent nature it was mooted that she should be executed whilst secured to a chair. In order to facilitate this unusual execution the pit beneath the gallows was to be widened to give room for the chair. In the end, however, Cotton, wearing a coarse black and white checked shawl, walked resignedly to her fate.

Following the post-mortem a plaster cast was taken of her face and she was buried in the western part of Durham prison at 2 pm. Having murdered her own mother, most of her children, the occasional lover and three husbands, Mary Ann Cotton, a former Sunday school teacher and nurse, will be remembered as one of the most prolific murderesses in British criminal history. She certainly made it in the playground:

Mary Ann Cotton, she's dead and forgotten,
She lies in a grave with her bones all rotten;
Sing, sing what shall we sing
Mary Ann Cotton's tied up with string.
Where, where? up in the air
Sellin black puddens a penny a pair

Mary Ann Cotton
dead and she's rotten
She lies in her bed
With her eyes wide open
Sing sing, oh, what can I sing?
Mary Ann Cotton is tied up with string.
Where, where? up in the air
Sellin black puddens a penny a pair

73. *Mary Ann Cotton, the region's most infamous murderess, poisoned her husbands, children and own mother. The total number of her victims is not known but is probably in the region of twenty.*

MOSTLY MURDER

MARWOOD - EXECUTIONER

HORRIBLE SCENE AT AN EXECUTION-DURHAM.

74. The botched execution of James Burton in 1883. The rope got tangled with his arm and the noose slipped over his chin. He was hauled out by the rope and violently shoved back into the pit.

GONE FOR A BURTON

Whatever their crime, nobody deserves to die like James Burton. The 33-year-old's life was a rather messy affair but as nothing when compared to his degrading death.

On 10th January, 1883, James tied the knot with 18-year-old Elizabeth Ann Sharpe at Tunstall in Sunderland. The young bride was not overenamoured with married life and just over one hundred days later left James to go into service. Whether Elizabeth had discovered her 'husband' was a bigamist, or whether she simply decided that the semi-slavery of service was infinitely preferable to the abject slavery of marriage is unrecorded. At all events the couple were soon living apart and James Burton was far from happy about the situation.

Some two weeks after their separation Burton met his 'wife' on the road close to a bridge near Silksworth Colliery. Elizabeth was wearing her best clothes: grey jacket, black dress and hat trimmed with velvet. She also sported a small umbrella. It is not known whether the rendezvous had been prearranged or Burton had been lying in wait for his estranged 'bride' but one thing is certain, Elizabeth was not dressed for the part she would soon have to play.

At 8.30 that same spring evening a passer-by witnessed a frenzied chase. A young woman was desperately evading the attentions of an older man. Indeed Elizabeth Burton was driven to such frantic measures to escape the clutches of her demented spouse, that she leapt over the railway and scrambled up the embankment. Badly hampered by her crinolines, the wretched girl was eventually captured as she neared the top of the slag heap. A desperate life and death struggle ensued. Suddenly the assailant picked up an unidentified object and the couple disappeared from view.

Elizabeth's body was later found in a shallow ditch. Large stones covered her head and feet and hips. Death was due to a blow to the base of the skull, probably delivered by a blunt instrument, certainly with great force. An absence of dirt in the wounds eliminated the likelihood of accidental death..

As in so many similar cases of the time, the guilty party attempted suicide prior to his arrest. Burton took an overdose of laudanum and later attempted to hang himself. He bungled both jobs and was subsequently arrested. Had he known what fate awaited him he would surely have taken greater care to get it right first time.

The trial, little more than a formality, resulted in the jury returning a guilty verdict after twenty-three minutes of deliberation. Burton was carried back to his cell in a semi-conscious state.

Whilst awaiting execution, the condemned man spent his time exercising, conversing with the prison chaplain and reading religious tracts. He made a full confession to Elizabeth Sharpe's parents on the 5th August 1883, the day before his execution:

I was blind at the time with passion, and I picked up a stone and hit her with it and she fell down in the same place where the body was picked up.

His last words were *Lord have mercy on my soul.* The Lord was not, however, in a merciful mood. What happened next is described by a local reporter:

[The] culprit walked firmly to the scaffold but on being placed in position looked up at the cross beam and on those assembled around the scaffold. Marwood at once placed the white cap over the culprit's face, fastened his legs and fixed the rope.

Immediately the bolt was drawn it was obvious something had gone wrong – the body was swinging violently to and fro in the pit. Marwood seized hold of the rope, and, assisted by a warder, dragged the still living man out of the pit. When drawn up Burton presented a shocking appearance. He was doubled up and it was seen that the rope had got entangled underneath his arm which had also allowed the noose to slip over his chin.

The white cap was partially removed, and it was observed that the culprit was still alive and bleeding. Marwood, having again placed the rope in position, pushed him violently into the pit. The body swayed backwards and forwards fully a couple of minutes and death must have been a painful one. The drop given was seven feet ten inches.

The following day the jury viewed the body at the coroner's court. It presented a ghastly appearance with the neck extremely swollen and face badly discoloured following a violent and painful death caused by strangulation by hanging.

A doctor told the court that the deceased man fainted on the drop, falling to one side. The rope caught his elbow so he was dragged out of the pit and put on his seat at the edge of the pit whilst the rope was disentangled by Marwood and the man then dropped down again. The coroner's jury posed just two questions:

Q: *Was he lifted out by the arm or by the rope?*
A: *By the rope.*
Q: *Do you consider the hangman was sober?*
A: *Yes, I think so.*

MURDER!

WANTED on suspicion of causing the death of a girl named **Lizzie Cavers Hogg Bucham,** on SATURDAY NIGHT, 26th MAY, at GOSFORTH, a man answering to the following description :—

About 30 to 35 years of age, 5 feet 7 or 8 inches high, proportionate build, dark complexion, thin pale face, moustache, but no whiskers, dressed in dark greasy cloth jacket, with blue cotton jacket underneath, and black glossy cap with peak, has the appearance of a Mechanic, Engine Driver, Fireman, or Machineman.

This man returned to Newcastle from Gosforth late on Saturday Night, the 26th May.

Any person who knows anyone answering to the above description, who had been keeping company with the deceased, is requested to immediately inform the Police.

All employers of labour, lodging house keepers, proprietors of lodgings, and others in Newcastle, Gateshead, and the neighbourhood, are earnestly requested to do the same ; especially if any lodger answering to the description came home late under suspicious circumstances on the night of the 26th May, or has left his employment since that date.

The man seen with Lizzie Bucham can clearly be identified if he can be found.

Any information should also be given to CAPTAIN TERRY, Chief Constable, Morpeth ; to the DETECTIVE DEPARTMENT, Newcastle ; or to myself,

ROBERT SPRATT,
CONSTABULARY OFFICE,   SUPERINTENDENT.
   GOSFORTH,
      30th May, 1894.

Tyne Printing Works Co., 26, Side, Newcastle-on-Tyne.

75. Rumours spread following two brutal murders that Jack the Ripper was at work in the North-East.

THE GOSFORTH TRAGEDY

A double murder in 1894 had locals talking about a northern Jack the Ripper. Walter Buchan, father of the girl in the wanted poster had the distressing task of formally identifying the body of his 18-year-old daughter. She had left home some seven days previously without leaving any forwarding address. Many witnesses came forward to say they had seen her eating stale bread and drinking with the man described in the poster. She was discovered stabbed to death following a severe kicking to the head.

Later that same year another woman died of similar wounds. Once again a description of a working man in his thirties was obtained by the police who believed the murders may have been connected. 32-year-old Anne Harland was known to the police as a prostitute. Her body was found on Town Moor a frequenting place for working girls. However neither of the two victims had been sexually assaulted. A boy found a knife near the scene but was spotted and questioned by a man as to what he intended to do with it. When told he meant to pass it on to the police the mystery man took the weapon and said that he would hand it in. Neither man nor knife were seen again. Two men were arrested as a result of the poster but both had alibis. By the end of the year there had still been no arrest and it appeared likely that, as with the London Ripper, the killer would not be brought to justice.

THE NOOSE PREFERABLE TO PENTONVILLE

One of Sunderland's most notorious prostitutes, 31-year-old Maria Fitzsimmons, was stabbed ten times by a visiting ship's cook, Thomas Fury, who managed to evade capture. Thirteen years later, having changed his name to Cort, Fury was sentenced to fifteen years on an unrelated charge of robbery and attempted murder. Conditions were so harsh in Pentonville that he determined to play the ultimate gamble – own up to a murder and then plead 'not guilty' at the last moment to elicit sympathy from the court. The jury were having none of it and Fury/Cort was sentenced to hang some thirteen years after his bloody night out in the North-East.

An intelligent man, he threw his defence notes, containing details of his early life, to the press at the end of the trial. He wrote: *As for me, I was a raving drunk before I'd reached my eighth birthday, and repeatedly drunk by the time I was ten*. Having spent thirteen years in prison he stated that he had met just one man inside whose crime had not been committed whilst under the influence. He spent his last days reading and writing as his executioner, Marwood, quaffed a few ales in the Dun Cow Inn.

Following a breakfast of toast, jam and tea a sober Thomas Fury was hanged on 16th May 1882. He wore the prison garb from Pentonville and showed no fear whatsoever of the hangman, asking if he could make a final address on the scaffold. Permission was refused.

ATTEMPTED MURDER AT GATESHEAD

Many apparently motiveless murders or attempted murders were followed by a suicide attempt. In 1878 John Lodge, a brickmaker, lived in Gateshead with his sister, Isabella, who acted as his housekeeper. At 1 am on a February morning a policeman, on routine beat, stumbled across a woman lying near some brick kilns. She was wearing only a chemise and petticoat. Both garments were drenched with blood which was gushing from her slashed throat. Isabella Lodge was barely conscious and in no condition to answer questions. Recognising the distraught victim, the policeman scooped her up and carried her the short distance to her house. Here he almost tripped over a second blood-smeared body, which was lying face-down on the

BEFORE THE MURDER | THE SUNDERLAND TRAGEDY | THE DISCOVERY

76. It was far easier to get away with murder if the victim was a prostitute. Thomas Fury was hanged after confessing to the murder of Maria Fitzsimmons thirteen years after the event.

ATTEMPTED MURDER AND SUICIDE AT GATESHEAD.

kitchen floor. This one was stone dead. A razor lay on the table.

John Lodge had been depressed for over a week and, determined to end his life, had decided to take his sister with him. He had tried to kill her as she lay in bed but, despite several slash wounds to her hands and face, Isabella managed to escape.

The coroner's court determined that Lodge had committed suicide whilst of unsound mind. Isabella was not expected to recover from her injuries.

BARKING MAD

The most reported murders have traditionally been those where the perpetrator has been convicted and 'taken a leap in the dark'. Many lesser-known murderers were of unsound mind and confined to asylums at her Majesty's pleasure.

A typical such case occurred in broad daylight in Newcastle, October 1861 in Blackett Street, outside the tax-office. Here Mark Frater, a well-respected tax collector was viciously stabbed by a man seemingly possessed. The killer not only thrust the dagger into his victim's neck but wrenched it around with such force that the blade became twisted. Frater stumbled through the door of his office and somehow managed to say to his clerk: *I'm afraid I'm done for.* Ten minutes later he was dead.

Meanwhile the knife-wielder, who had made no attempt to escape, was easily contained by two passers-by. When finally the killer stood before the judge he appeared to be overjoyed at his actions, enthusiastically admitting guilt and declaring:

Decidedly so, decidedly so; I've murdered him; he robbed me and now I've robbed him. This is a grand job for the penny papers; they'll have a rare sale to-day.

The prisoner, Clark, tried at the assizes and sentenced to hang, was ultimately reprieved and sent to howl at the moon for the rest of his natural. His motive? Six months previously he had refused to pay the dog tax and Frater had seized goods to the value.

THE LOW BRIDGE MURDER

31-year-old John Fenning's marriage lasted just six months before his wife packed her bags and went home to mum. In court some months later, despite his loud protestations, the fitter was ordered to pay his estranged spouse five shillings per week. The normally sedate and sober husband was ushered out of the courtroom threatening the life of the woman who, only a year before, had been his main reason to live.

As time passed, the more inebriated and maudlin he became, the more vicious his threats grew. On the afternoon of November 26th, 1886 Fenning visited pubs in the area where his wife and her mother lodged. During the evening he was twice repulsed when trying to break into his mother-in-law's home. He eventually left the scene between 9 and 10 pm.

78. Pink Lane, Newcastle in 1899. Here some thirteen years earlier, a man with murderous intentions picked up prostitute Annie Richardson.

The prosecution later argued that he subsequently went to visit women *of the most depraved character* and where better to find them than at Low Bridge? Fenning quickly fell into conversation with a known prostitute in a Pink Lane public house. The deal struck, Annie Richardson invited the punter back to her place in Blythe Nook, Cowgate. William Baker her landlord, however, wanted no nooky on his premises and refused to allow the couple to complete their transaction. Doubly thwarted and increasingly obsessed with that morning's court ruling against him, Fenning produced a black-handled cut-throat razor and graphically described to the landlord what he was going to do to those who should have been his nearest and dearest. He then stomped off into the night.

Around midnight he was seen to approach Elizabeth Tait, who was working the night shift on Dean Street. Refused entrance to number 15 Low Bridge the couple fell to bickering, an event overheard by the next door neighbour:

F: *I have not got it.*
M: *If you have not got it who could have got it?*

Street girls were renowned for pocketing drunken punters' watches and wallets and the neighbour

assumed that this is what Fenning and Tait were arguing about. The next moment cries of *police* and *murder* echoed through the deserted streets. All manner of semi-clad life forms descended to the chilly streets below where Elizabeth Tait lay bleeding to death, her throat and forehead deeply gashed. Several witnesses saw a man in dark clothes and a black 'pot hat' tearing up Low Bridge towards Pilgrim Street.

Drawn by a suspicious nature, a passing policeman stopped the fleeing man and asked for his address. The suspect gave his name as John Henry Fenning and even provided his correct address, 16 Prince's Street. When the gravity of the crime was appreciated police were despatched to Prince's Street and Fenning was arrested at 2 am. His hands, the cuffs of his shirt, the arms of his coat, the breast of his vest and the legs of his trousers were drenched in blood. Fenning remained silent throughout the process of his arrest.

In court a large number of witnesses testified to

79. The Side, Newcastle pre-1892 where Fenning made his escape following the fatal slashing of Elizabeth Tait.

having heard a dispute and seeing a man dressed in black but the evidence against Fenning was wholly circumstantial. No weapon was found and, more puzzlingly, no one could decide why anyone guilty of murder would give their correct address to the police?

Today most prosecutors are reluctant to call unreliable witnesses, who are often proved to be liars under cross-examination and tend therefore to hinder rather than help with conviction. To support their rather flimsy case the prosecutors turned to three gaolbirds, who shared a cell with Fenning. They testified that the accused had admitted to the murder whilst in police custody but their statements weakened rather than strengthened the prosecution's case.

Samuel Brindle told the court that he was on remand in Newcastle gaol for receiving three shillings. On the morning following the murder of Elizabeth Tait he had met Fenning in police custody and asked him what he was accused of. Fenning replied that he had *nearly cut a woman's head off in Newcastle*. The following conversation was then alleged to have taken place:

BRINDLE: *They have soon catched you then.*

80. Many Victorian murders followed the familiar pattern of a man slaying his wife/girlfriend and then attempting suicide. These roles were reversed in North Shields, September 1883. Early one Tuesday morning a policeman heard screams coming from a house in Clive Street. Forcing entry he found Frank Mendigo, an itinerant musician, bleeding heavily from a stab wound to his back. His wife, Eleanor, was lying close in a pool of her own blood. Both were rushed to hospital in a critical condition.

FENNING: *A policeman stopped me two or three minutes after I'd done it but he let me go again.*

BRINDLE: *How was that?*

FENNING: *I gave a false address. I gave 12, Pilgrim Street and it was 12, Princes Street.*

BRINDLE: *Is she a married woman as you've killed?*

FENNING: *No; she's a prostitute. I'd have killed the wife and all if they'd have given me time; for she's nothing but an adulterous prostitute.*

BRINDLE: *Did they find a knife on you then?*

FENNING: *No, it wasn't a knife I did it with; it was a very sharp chisel I'd sharpened for the purpose.*

Defence attorney cast strong doubt onto the truthfulness of the above conversation when he elicited that Brindle, an ex-policeman, had been imprisoned for false pretences. A second man on remand *for helping a man to carry a bundle* told yet another contradictory story. Altogether the men's stories did not hold water.

The defence, summing up, stressed that Fenning was previously of good character and the evidence against him purely circumstantial. Following thirty-five minutes of deliberation, the jury agreed.

Fenning's acquittal was probably down to two things: the victim was an unfortunate (prostitute), considered by the hypocritical all-male jury to be the lowest form of life. More importantly, however, Fenning's work colleagues paid for the services of a good defence attorney.

Throughout his six week ordeal the defendant's cash-strapped mother had sent him tea. Following her son's acquittal, she was pleasantly surprised to discover a 1lb. pack of tea on her doorstep from an anonymous well-wisher.

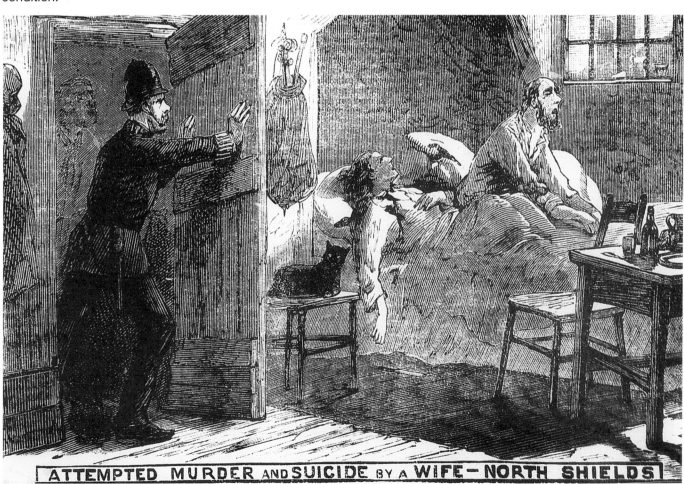

ATTEMPTED MURDER AND SUICIDE BY A WIFE – NORTH SHIELDS

SHOCKING MURDER IN NEWCASTLE

81. It was far easier to get away with murder if the victim was a prostitute. In November 1869 George Weirs, a fireman on the screw steamer 'Fusilier', spent some two hours with the 'unfortunate' Matilda Martin. At 2 a.m. the screams of murder pierced the air. As a policeman made his way to the scene he passed a man who insisted he had been robbed. Matilda was found lying on the flags, bleeding profusely from a wound in the left breast. She died from her wounds some fifteen minutes later. It appeared she had been caught attempting to pick a punter's pocket and paid the ultimate penalty. There was not enough evidence against Weirs and Matilda's death was put down to wilful murder but by whom there is not sufficient evidence to prove.

BREAK-IN AT THE VICARAGE

The planting of false evidence, principally by the police, has been a problem since trials were conceived. How many innocent people have gone down because a shortage of hard evidence has necessitated its fabrication?

Peter Murphy and Michael Brannagan had served seven years of a life sentence before an investigation proved beyond doubt that all of the evidence against them was invented by the Northumberland Constabulary.

In 1879, during the early hours of the 7th February, the back doors of the vicarage of Edlingham – a small village some five miles S.W. of Alnwick – were jemmied open with a chisel. Two intruders gained access and began fumbling and foraging in the dark, unfamiliar surroundings. They made too much noise for professional thieves and woke Georgina Buckle, who immediately informed her father of the clattering downstairs.

Mr Buckle, at 77, was still a fit man. He armed himself with a heavy sword and father and daughter edged their way gingerly down the stairs. Arriving on the ground floor they cast caution to the wind and brazenly breached the drawing room which was temporarily illuminated by the candle held high in Mr Buckle's left hand.

As in all battles exactly what happened next is unclear. The flame was swiftly extinguished as the plucky clergyman was pushed aside. In the darkness Mr Buckle swung his sword blindly and made contact with the intruders, if not with their flesh then at least with their clothes. His weapon was later shown to be blunt. It would not have drawn blood.

But blood was certainly drawn a few seconds later as a single shot from a scatter gun sent the Buckles reeling to the floor. Both were bleeding profusely. Father Buckle took four grains of shot to the shoulder. Georgina, however, was more seriously injured, she'd been shot in the groin. With the Buckles lying shocked, bloodied and clutching their wounds, the two intruders escaped via the window. They landed on a soft mound of soil and sped off in the direction of Alnwick.

Help quickly arrived and, as father and daughter had their wounds dressed, Superintendent Harkes surveyed

83. Mr Buckle's blunt sword was no match for the burglars' scatter gun. Had either the clergyman or his daughter succumbed to their wounds, two innocent men may well have hanged.

82. Edlingham Rectory, scene of the shooting of Father and daughter Buckle that led to a gross miscarriage of justice.

the scene of crime. Only one item, Georgina's watch, was found to be missing. A chisel and newspaper found outside the dining room door were passed on to the man leading the inquiry. Both would become important as the case proceeded. As day dawned, more evidence came to light in the form of shoe and hand prints in the garden.

The botched burglary was almost certainly a local job and police targeted known villains and poachers living in nearby Alnwick. 44-year-old Michael Brannagan and Peter Murphy, roughly half his age, were stopped on the outskirts of town at 7 am the morning of the shootings. Detecting them had been easy. They'd been out all night so were obviously guilty of something. As far as the police were concerned, they had their men and, if the evidence didn't fit, they would soon make it.

After being stopped, both labourers were escorted home. Scarcely had he removed his clogs than Brannagan was arrested. Murphy had just enough time to change out of his wet clothes before he too was taken into custody. In a desperate effort to help her man, his fiancee, Agnes, examined his coat pockets and to her horror discovered evidence of a crime: blood and fur she knew came from a rabbit. Fearing her beau would be sent down for poaching, she swiftly cut out the incriminating pockets and hid the coat. When asked to produce the clothes Murphy had worn that night, she handed over a jacket that belonged to another member of the household, Murphy's brother-in-law, a man named Redpath.

At the police station, literally swearing their innocence, both part-time poachers were roughly stripped and clumsily examined. Neither man's clothes nor bodies showed any recent contact with a sword, but later in court a doctor would testify that the skin of Murphy's neck gave the appearance of having been bruised with a blunt instrument.

Murphy and Brannagan were then paraded at the scene of crime but could not be positively identified by the Buckles. In the light of this and with no evidence whatsoever the police proceeded with the prosecution. If the facts were missing they could always be created.

At a preliminary hearing, plaster casts of footmarks, allegedly made by the intruders on a path leading to Alnwick Road, were produced. The casts matched the prisoners' boots and clogs, which had been confiscated by the police. Detectives also managed to trick Murphy's brother-in-law, Redpath, into saying that the chisel found at the scene of crime belonged to him. They did this by adding it to his box of tools and asking him if they were his. Redpath, who had defective eyesight, confirmed the chisel was his, the inference being that Murphy had stolen it.

The indisputable evidence of a set-up, however, was a scrap of newspaper found in 'Murphy's' jacket – the one his fiancee had switched. The fragment of paper was discovered more than a week after the crime by the highly-respected doctor who had treated the Buckles. The torn piece of paper fitted the newspaper found at the scene of crime. It looked like the final piece of a jig-saw. No one commented on the fact that both the 'Murphy's' switched jacket and the newspaper had been in the possession of the police from day one.

At the trial the police wanted to produce some more fabricated evidence which we shall reveal later, though the judge would not admit it into evidence.

After being unable to identify his assailants the day following his attack, Mr Buckle, perhaps with a little prompting from the police, suddenly regained his memory and was now certain that the two men in the dock were guilty. Whether the clergyman deliberately broke the ninth commandment only he (and his Maker) could know. One thing is clear, his Christian, or possibly guilty conscience was evidenced towards the end of the trial when he asked for leniency to be shown the two defendants.

Throughout the trial the defence pulled no punches. From the outset, they argued that the police, in order to improve their detection rates, had entirely fabricated the evidence. Mr Milvain reasoned that any number of people would have milled around the vicarage before and after the crime. He contended that no distinct footmarks had been discovered beneath the drawing-room window at the early stages of the investigation, and tore into the newspaper 'evidence', emphasising the length of time it had taken for the fragment of paper to be discovered.

During the hearing several witnesses stated that they had never seen Redpath with the chisel on exhibit, and further declared that although the accused were well-known poachers, they had never been known to carry firearms, preferring instead to using *a clever terrier* to find rabbits. It also emerged that following their arrest, the accused men had admitted that on the night in question they had been rabbiting with their dog and had subsequently hidden their prey. Police stated that an officer had in fact found the rabbits in the place the suspects said. The animals had not been shot.

Despite conflicting evidence, and following a one-sided summation in favour of the prosecution, the jury deliberated for three hours before returning a guilty verdict. To a background of loud protestations, both from the public galleries and the men themselves, both were sentenced to life imprisonment. In those days 'life' meant a minimum of twenty years. There can be no doubt that had either of the Buckles succumbed to their injuries before sentence was pronounced, the convicted men would have hanged.

After passing through Pentonville and Millbank, Brannagan was sent to Dartmoor and Murphy to Portsmouth. On the way to Pentonville one of the escorting officers offered £10 if the prisoners revealed the hiding place of Georgina's stolen watch. In response Brannagan could only assert the truth:

I was never near the place.

Upon arrival at Pentonville, Murphy produced a lock of his sweetheart's hair and asked the senior warder whether he could keep it. He was met by a blunt refusal:

Decidedly not; put it in your clothes and the old Jew will get it to-morrow when he comes round for clothing.

At Pentonville the clothing of convicts incarcerated for lengthy periods was sold.

Throughout his sentence Murphy wrote every three months to his fiancee protesting his innocence. His letters, currently kept by the Gosforth Record Office, show that he found God in a big way. In a letter to his sister Mary Ann at Shields Yard, Clayport Street, Alnwick in August 1881 Peter Murphy seemed certain of divine intervention:

I want you to bear in mind in the first place that I am an innocent man suffering for the evil deeds of others which I hope and trust you all believe so it's very hard for me to be in good spirits...I feel sure in my heart that the almighty God will bring us to justice soon there is never a man in prison innocent but always something turns up for him.

Two years later, in a letter to Agnes, Peter Murphy asked her not to come and see him as it would only make him feel worse.

Life continued at its usual slow pace. Seven years passed. In small communities everyone knows everyone else's business and inevitably the story of the 'Alnwick Two' continued to do the rounds: it would simply not die as it surely would have had they been guilty.

Had it not been for the interest shown in the case by the young vicar of St. Paul's in Alnwick, Brannagan and Murphy might simply have wasted away in prison. Father Jevon J Muschamp Perry had heard whispers and gossip, perhaps even prayers, and he determined to prove the truth of the crime.

In order to secure the release of Murphy and

Brannagan, Perry had to ferret out the true perpetrators of the Edlingham Vicarage crime. A popular rumour doing the rounds was that George Edgell, 47, had been 'out' on the night of the break-in. When Perry directly confronted Edgell as to his movements on 8th February 1879, the poacher became very distressed and agitated. According to Perry, Edgell literally shook with terror, turned as pale as death and gasped for breath. He called out for water and, when refreshed and a little calmer, denied doing the shooting.

As time wore on the poacher could take no more gossip, finger-pointing and priestly interrogations and eventually he made a full confession to the vicar. He said that his accomplice that night, seven years previously, was one of the hardest and strongest men in the whole county. Charles Richardson, 53, was well known to the police as he was thought to be one of three men responsible for the murder of Constable George Grey at Eglingham in 1873. At the time there had been insufficient evidence to convict him.

The Eglingham murder had taken place in the early hours of a Saturday night in January. P.C. Grey, the father of five and with seven years in the force, stumbled across three men on the road to Old Bewicke. They appeared to be carrying firearms and, upon seeing the officer, they sought to hide in a field of turnips. Grey, believing the men to be either poachers or burglars, vaulted the hedge and pursued them through the turnip field. The men were stopped in their tracks by a net, stretched out to prevent sheep straying into the field. Two of the men then turned on their unarmed pursuer and discharged their weapons, probably scatter-guns. Shots pierced all parts of the policeman's body, from neck to his groin. Twenty small shots were even found to have passed through Grey's belt. Despite the severity of his injuries, the wounded man managed to drag himself some twenty yards to Glebe Cottage from which help was summoned. Grey died at five o'clock that same Saturday afternoon, shortly after Archdeacon Hamilton gave him the last rights and took his final deposition. A local collection for his widow and children raised an impressive £84 and Eglingham church was filled to overflowing the next week with distraught villagers wishing to pay their last respects.

In one of his depositions Grey named one of the men he believed had shot him – a returned convict named Schofield. The suspect was found and promptly arrested in Newcastle and later transferred to Alnwick. Here another suspect, Charles Richardson, was already under arrest. A verdict of wilful murder by three men unknown was returned in the coroner's court but no evidence could be produced against the two men in custody who were consequently released.

From Eglingham in 1873 we return to the break-in at Edlingham, 1879.

The truth of that fateful night at the vicarage in Edlingham took seven years to surface, but was finally divulged to the persistent Reverend Perry.

Following an unsuccessful night's poaching Edgell and Richardson determined not to return home empty-handed. It was Richardson's idea to break into the Buckle's vicarage and he who forced entry, using a chisel

84. *Alnwick, the home town dreamed about in prison by Brannagan and Murphy wrongly sentenced to life imprisonment.*

stolen from an out-house. The only object taken was Georgina Buckle's gold watch which had a trinket – a gilt eagle – attached to the chain. Richardson sold the tiny bird to a jeweller who would later testify against him. The watch itself had been too hot to handle and a reluctant Richardson had thrown it into the Tyne.

The news of Edgell's confession was passed on to Mr Milvain, the lawyer who had defended Brannagan and Murphy and was now the Recorder of Durham. He immediately persuaded the Home Secretary to commission an enquiry.

Happily news of these events filtered through to the two men inside. Brannagan later recalled the moment he received his wife's letter saying that two other men had confessed to the crime for which he had been incarcerated:

I chucked my dinner on one side. I could not eat it and I had to get up and walk about a bit. That night my heart was thumping awful and I did not sleep.

Events speeded up from this point on and the men were soon reprieved. Upon release Brannagan managed to smoke a pipe of cut tobacco, but Murphy, after a few pulls, was rendered sick and did not think he would touch beer or baccy again. Brannagan seemed to have aged badly in prison, but Murphy, who had found religion, seemed young and vigorous. But the prison fare caused unforeseen problems: their first feast of roast pork left Murphy waxing lyrical over the best beef he'd eaten in years!

They were accompanied home on the train by reporters who themselves were overcome with emotion:

At Bilton Station over a score of people were present to witness the arrival of the emancipated men. Amongst them were the sisters of Murphy, and his brother-in-law, and their meeting was so emotional that we shall draw a curtain over the feelings displayed and leave to be imagined the depth of heartfelt joy and gladness overflowing in their bosoms.

Both men's pardons were signed by Queen Victoria and they each received £800 in compensation from the treasury. The two were offered £15 plus expenses to appear on stage for a few minutes, but both declined the offer and settled into employment at the skills they had learnt inside: Brannagan as wheelwright and Murphy as baker. Murphy later married the faithful Agnes Simms.
With the two wronged men safely back in the bosom of their local communities, the case against Edgell and Richardson began.

UNFINISHED BUSINESS

When the true perpetrators of the Edlingham Vicarage incident were finally convicted, they received peculiarly lenient sentences: five years each. Perhaps the judiciary was still reeling from the embarrassment of Murphy and Brannagan. Whatever the cause, five years was a remarkably light sentence for Richardson. It had been he, after all, who had twice discharged his scatter gun. He had fired at two innocent people who were merely attempting to protect their own home and in all likelihood he had also fired the same gun at the hapless Constable Gray. In the face of these facts and suspicion, five years was a very soft sentence for the hard man of Alnwick.

Of greater interest were the later allegations of planting by the police. And at this point the evidence which the judge at Murphy and Brannagan's trial deemed inadmissible now came to light.

According to 1879 police reports, exactly one month after the Edlingham Vicarage break-in, a zealous police-officer returned to the scene of the crime and 'discovered' under the drawing-room window, a piece of fustian cloth with a button attached. Amazingly enough, after one month in the mud and snow, the evidence was fresh and clean. This fabric exactly fitted a hole in Brannagan's trousers. This material evidence, according to the police, had been torn from Brannagan's breeches as he made good his escape. A tailor would later state that in his opinion the piece of corduroy looked more cut than torn.

We don't really know why the judge ordered that the piece of fabric be withheld from evidence. We do however know that the deliberate planting and falsification of evidence in the Murphy/Brannagan case was investigated by a Scotland Yard detective. In the absence of Superintendent Harks, who had been in charge of the original case but had since died, Inspector Butcher recommended that a criminal prosecution

MICHAEL BRANNAGAN.

85   PETER MURPHY.

should be taken out against Harks' four constables: Harrison, Sprott, Gair and Chambers.

The four officers were consequently charged with making false plaster casts of footprints; entrapping Redpath into a mistaken recognition of the chisel; tearing a piece of newspaper found in the vicarage and feloniously placing it in the lining of what they believed to be Murphy's coat and finally, of tearing or cutting a piece of cloth from Brannagan's trousers in order to prove that he had been at the scene of the crime. A verdict of *not guilty for want of proof* was returned. The constables were only 'obeying orders'.

We will never know if one of them would have broken rank if either of the Buckles had died and two innocent men faced the drop.

'A CHAPTER OF ACCIDENTS'

86. *Spectators watching the fire in Gateshead from the bridge had to flee for cover when an enormous explosion heard as far away as Hartlepool sent massive fire balls crashing down north of the river.*

THE GREAT FIRE OF GATESHEAD

The 'Pudding Lane' of the Great Fire of Newcastle and Gateshead was a row of factories south of the Tyne. Unfortunately the source of the blaze was not a humble bakery but a worsted factory, whose many heavy machines continually dripped oil onto the wooden floor.

Once the fire took hold, around midnight on 5th October 1854, the building was completely gutted within the hour. More worryingly, the flames had caught the surrounding buildings, including one of the largest structure on the river front, the seven-storey Bertram's warehouse. This stone-built construction had been double fire-proofed because of the unstable nature of the contents in storage. So fierce was the nearby blaze, however, that the flames easily overcame all defences and ripped through the building. The stock within included 200 tons of iron; 800 tons of lead; 170 tons of manganese; 130 tons of nitrate of soda; 3,000 tons of brimstone; 4,000 tons of guano; 10 tons of alum; 5 tons of arsenic; 30 tons of copperas; one ton of naphtha and 240 tons of salt. It was the largest lethal firecracker on the Tyne.

Fifty soldiers were immediately dispatched from Newcastle to help badly overstretched firemen in their losing battle against the inferno. By 3 am most of the inhabitants on the Newcastle side of the river were staring in awe as vivid blue flames rapidly threatened to consume surrounding houses. Meanwhile the citizens of Gateshead were rapidly evacuating their properties.

Shortly after 3 am a minor explosion was followed by the loudest ear-shattering blast ever heard in the north. It was so loud it was heard in Hexham and Hartlepool and by trawlermen twenty miles off the coast. A local journalist wrote: *The air was rent as by the voice of many thunders and filled as with the spume of a volcano.* Both Gateshead and Newcastle trembled as if in an earthquake and indeed the keels on the Tyne were almost blown out of the water. Bertram's warehouse was a live volcano spewing out burning balls of brimstone, brick, rocks and red-hot metal. The best contemporary description of this scene of destruction and mayhem comes from the *Nonconformist*:

Massive walls were crumbled into heaps – blocks of houses tumbled into ruin – windows shattered from their frames far and near – gravestones broken and uplifted as if the trumpet of resurrection had sounded – a livid corpse was hurled across the river and a shower of burning timbers and crashing stones rained terror, death and destruction all around.

As the fire took hold of properties north of the river, large stones and fireballs were catapulted into homes throughout Newcastle, causing pandemonium to those who, a few minutes earlier, had been mere passive onlookers.

The largest 'bombs' landed in Gateshead with one big boulder smashing the roof of the Grey Horse public house nearly a quarter-of-a-mile from the seat of the explosion. Another projectile, nearly 4ft long and weighing a staggering 4cwt embedded itself in a street in Oakwellgate. Many of the gravestones in St. Mary's Church were removed by the force of the explosion and thrown a considerable distance, crashing walls to rest in pieces in some adjoining houses.

Meanwhile back in Newcastle the sky was alight with burning wood and red hot stones, which rained down on buildings some three-quarters of a mile from the warehouse. Both the Ridley Arms and Blue Post inns in Ridley Street were badly damaged. A stone, weighing 18lbs, that embedded itself in the floor of a workshop in Grey Street, was still too hot to be handled by the time workers arrived hours later.

The worst hit area was Quayside, where lighted missiles had landed on three houses. The flames had spread with lightening speed, shattering the glass of shop fronts and extinguishing the gas lights. Noxious gasses penetrated the lungs of panic-stricken spectators who were now involved in the drama. All around the streets were sprayed with vomit where people became sick following the inhalation of sulphur fumes.

A second contemporary account captures the mayhem, panic and sheer terror:

Men, women and children were rushing about in their night-dresses without knowing where they were going; mothers were vainly endeavouring to enter their falling houses to recover their children; children were seeking their parents; here was a husband trying to find his wife and five children. Many who had just before been seen assisting to subdue the flames had disappeared among the falling debris...The ground near the explosion was strewed with the bodies of the dead and the dying and the wounded.

The fifty soldiers took the full force of the blast and, of the thirty immediately struck down, two died on the spot, one in a most horrific manner, of an iron bar deeply penetrating his body. Firemen and volunteers at the seat of the blaze died instantly. Now unopposed, the inferno raged unchecked throughout the night and by the following morning there were fears that both towns would be razed to the ground.

All neighbouring towns were telegraphed for assistance and help was swiftly dispatched from

87. *Approximately 53 people died as massive walls crumbled into heaps and blocks of houses tumbled into ruin. One local reporter asserted that a corpse was hurled across the river in the blast.*

Sunderland, Hexham, Durham, Morpeth and Berwick. Exhausted smoke-stained locals were replaced by fresh volunteers. The fire was finally brought under control by the 7th October.

The grisly search for bodies and injured survivors could now begin. Bricks and rubble were still red-hot and volunteers had their boots burnt off their feet. Over a hundred injured people were carried to the infirmary on boards and window shutters. Fifteen quickly succumbed to their injuries.

Many of the bodies were barely recognisable and these corpses had to be identified by those personal possessions that had not burnt or melted in the intense heat. In Gateshead a piece of coat and a bunch of keys assisted in the identification of John Dobson's second son. Thomas Sharp's relations recognised his gold watch and two dog whistles. A Mr Davidson was identified by his signet ring, whilst a cigar case clinched the identification of Mr Harrison. One of the firemen was recognised by the nozzle of the hose pipe he had been training on the fire. The whole Hart family perished in Churchwalk and as for Mr Bertram himself, not one portion of him was found; his death was confirmed when his key and snuff box were discovered among the debris of his warehouse.

Where there are fatalities, there are narrow escapes. The superintendent of Gateshead police, Mr Schorey, blown off his feet in the blast, landed under an archway which sheltered him from falling debris. Another policeman, Superintendent Dunne, leapt from a burning building seconds before it collapsed. Mrs Redpath, Keeper of the Guildhall, left her bed seconds before it was submerged beneath a collapsed brick wall. A married couple in Oakwellgate saw their recently-vacated bed crushed by a large stone that had smashed through the roof.

An unforeseen consequence of the fire was the enormous influx of people from the surrounding villages and towns who came to witness the devastation. The following Friday the streets of Newcastle thronged as on Fair days and, by Saturday over 20,000 people had arrived in the city by train alone. Special trains ran every hour and so great was the demand that many punters waited hours at their stations before being able to board. Some came to see if their families were safe, others to grieve, but most were simple sightseers. Inhaling the noxious polluted air, they gleefully picked their way through charred ruins, all the while shaking their heads in feigned horror and genuine disbelief.

All in all, an estimated 53 lives were lost and over £1 million worth of damage done. At the inquests into the deaths, inevitable questions as to the causes of the explosion were asked. After lengthy testimony by top chemists of the day, open verdicts were returned, though the juries agreed that they believed gunpowder had played no part in the explosion.

88. Quayside two weeks before the fire in 1854.

89. *Quayside after the fire.*

THE SUNDERLAND TRAGEDY

In the Summer of 1883, Mr Fay toured the schools of Sunderland drumming up an audience for his forthcoming show. He promised that every child would have a chance of receiving a present after the event, which he billed as 'The Greatest Treat Ever Given For Children'. It was to be held at the Victoria Hall.

Having set the entrance fee at a mere 1d, so that as many children as possible could escape the often humdrum nature of their lives for a few exciting hours, when the day finally came two thousand spellbound children trooped into Victoria Hall. Entranced by Mr Fay's magic, boys and girls screamed with delight as he projected his voice across the stage. Wide-eyed and expectant, cheering and hissing at all the right times, the children were quickly absorbed by the fantastic world of the professional entertainer. Although one of Fay's turns, involving copious quantities of smoke, caused several children to vomit, he quickly won them back and the audience was in raptures as the final act saw Fay 'hatching' pigeons and allowing them to fly all around the hall. At 5.10 pm, with the performance now ended, the best was yet to come as far as the majority of the children were concerned: the giving out of presents. Presents were rare treats in the lives of most of those in attendance.

The Victoria Hall, situated on the corner of Toward Road and Murton Street, was split into three. The stalls seated about 1,000 people; the gallery had seating for 1,100 with room for about 400 more. On the afternoon in question, the upper circle was occupied by just one woman and her child, while the lower floors were full to bursting with excited children fantasising as to what present they would receive.

Mr Fay was a man of his word and, at the conclusion of his highly successful show he, along with his helpers, began throwing small treats to the delighted youngsters in the body of the hall. Each throw resulted in a scrummage as a beaming child secreted a gift, and others scampered for the next prize. The children in the gallery looked on in alarmed disbelief. No presents were coming their way. The action was all downstairs. Suddenly the words they had been waiting for came: *This way for prizes*.

Children nearest the upstairs exits, who heard the summons, quickly slipped out. They were followed down the flights of stairs by hundreds of frenzied followers desperate not to miss the promised freebies.

Whether the entrance to the body of the hall was locked we do not know. It may be that the doors were opened so that only one child at a time could pass through. At all events, a backlog soon occurred.

The first people on the scene believed that three children had tried to pass through together and became wedged in the doorway. A flood of children then tumbled head over heels, one on top of the other. Shrieks and screams resounded down the staircases until all air was squeezed from the tiny lungs.

But more still pressed down from above.
Mr Graham, the manager stated:

…When I approached the lower door I heard fearful screams, groans and noises of struggling. I rushed to the door and attempted to open it, and found I could not do so; the bolt was in the socket about two feet from the door frame, and the opening was jammed up nearly as high as my head with the bodies of children.

The manager hurtled his way upstairs by another route and came down stairways crammed with children:

…When we reached the fourth step from the bottom we found the children packed in a mass from that place over the whole of the landing below. There seemed to be hundreds of them. At first I did not think that any were dead, but when we came to attempt releasing them I discovered my mistake. I tried at first to take out children from the thickest of the mass, but they were so tightly wedged in that I could scarcely move them without risk of further injury to their poor limbs, so I began by picking out those little ones from the top who groaned, moved their limbs or showed other signs of life. Two gentlemen, one named Raine, quickly came to my assistance and we handed the injured children through the window or the door to a constable who ran with them to the porch of the building and placed them in the open air. We worked very hard, but the children were lying wedged together eight deep and it was difficult to get at them.

Some rather confused and contradictory statements were taken from the survivors. 12-year-old Thomas Wilson, who was at the back of the main hall, stated that a man on the stage told those downstairs that presents were available in the gallery. At the door a man was standing giving away prizes but when the donor saw a boy who had somehow got hold of five or six presents he said *this will never do* and proceeded to bolt the door. He then threw some prizes towards the street and told the children to leave via the Toward Road door. Thomas managed to acquire a round whistle and made his way home safely.

Those upstairs were not so lucky. Mr Simpson wrote to the local newspaper about his son's experiences:

My eldest boy was in the doomed gallery. His story of the tragedy is that before the close of the performance he thought he would leave as he had sense to know that there would be a crush in the ordinary egress. He descended the stairs a few minutes before the finish. When he came to the fatal door he found it shut and bolted. He tried to remove the bolt, but he could not, and before he knew down came the human mass on the top of him. How he was saved is a miracle to me. He felt as though he was falling asleep. He was carried out into the hall, and by kind aid and medical skill he was restored. Now if the door had been two foot open, and the bolt in to allow one to pass at a time, he would have gone straight out. The door had been shut and the bolt put down, and there was not a soul to guard or look after this in any way.

Nine-year-old George Howitt was also in the gallery, and, he too, left through a door which had been left some eighteen inches open. He watched as a man gave away prizes and then noticed that the door was only *a little bit open*. George had been sitting on a form with Frank and Emily Morris. Emily was killed and Frank fainted but later regained consciousness.

An 11-year-old, Inez Coe was indirectly spared because of her disability. She took to the stairs early to *avoid the crush* and was told by a man at the bottom of the stairs that she could not leave until the others from upstairs had come down. Once the stampede started, Inez snuggled into the corner and used her crutch as a crash-barrier. She saw a boy fall down and others trip over him and she squeezed into the corner as bodies piled up around her. After what must have seemed like hours, she saw a man reaching down to pull out the dead bodies that surrounded her. Screaming out *Take me out before the dead ones, I'm alive.* Inez was hoisted clear. On reaching the outside hall she fainted but was revived with a bucket of cold water.

The tragedy had such a traumatising effect on its survivors that ten years later, Sidney Duncan, aged ten at the time of the incident, could recall the events as if they had happened the previous day:

Within half a minute I was forced off my feet and almost buried in the struggling, dying mass. Only the cries of a few who were being crushed in the pack behind could be heard. In front comparative silence reigned but the writhings of the expiring little ones were fearful to behold. I witnessed all, and lay unable even to aid myself. Fully five minutes elapsed before assistance arrived.

From the contradictory statements it seems that, in the rush for presents both from the gallery and main hall, a member of staff must have bolted the door with the intention of keeping the two sectors of the audience apart. This action was to cost the people of Sunderland dear.

183 children (114 boys and 69 girls) were crushed or trampled to death and another 100 seriously injured. Most of the victims were aged between seven and ten, but two were just three-years-old. The mangled bodies, many barely recognisable, were laid out in rows for identification purposes. More than one family lost all of their children. A man and his wife anxiously scanned the rows of the dead. His face blanched and, without betraying any further sign of emotion, he pointed to a little figure, *that's one*. A few yards later he pointed again, *that's another*. Then, as he came to the last child in the row, he lost all composure and burst into loud sobs *My God! All my family gone.*

Queen Victoria wrote to the clergymen of the town, who relayed her message of condolence at the subsequent funerals and in services throughout the grief-stricken town.

Let's hope her words came true: *Suffer little children to come unto me, for of such is the kingdom of God.*

90. Scenes from the Sunderland tragedy that shocked the whole country.

TALES OF THE UNEXPECTED

91. Some actors reacted badly to criticism and doubled up as bouncers. Here Hamlet ejects a critic from the Theatre Royal, South Shields.

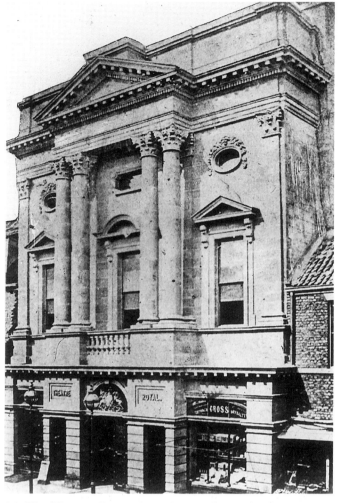

92. The Theatre Royal, King Street, South Shields c1866. Scene of Hamlet's revenge.

AN IRATE HAMLET AT THE SOUTH SHIELDS THEATRE ROYAL

Victorian theatre audiences were far more boisterous and disruptive than is the case today. If a play or show didn't please them they weren't averse to letting the players know in no uncertain terms. These attacks would usually be verbal in nature, but occasionally vegetables were thrown onto the stage and, if the 'entertainment' was deemed particularly poor, a full-scale riot might break out.

Good productions were also sometimes interrupted by drunken oafs, whom few found funny. In November, 1871, Mr Goddard Whyatt, lessee of the South Shields Theatre Royal, was playing the title role in Hamlet. As he was about to deliver the famous soliloquy commencing *To be, or not to be* the theatre was in total silence. Suddenly a drunkard in the gallery let forth a volley of oaths.

Goddard Whyatt, aka Hamlet, left Ophelia on the stage. He had not gone off to sulk, however, as the next the audience saw of him was sixty seconds later when he made an unscheduled entrance to the gallery, sword in hand.

With the assistance of irate members of the audience, he succeeded in ejecting the noisy 'god' from the theatre. On descending to the stage, amidst the deafening applause of the audience, he announced *Hamlet's himself again* and proceeded with the part.

FEARFUL POSITION OF A YOUNG GIRL

Many Newcastle streets were crisscrossed with lines of drying clothes. Ropes ran through pulleys fastened to the woodwork of opposite houses so clothes could be drawn to and fro at leisure. One day in the summer of 1878 young Lydia Stevens, whilst leaning out of a first floor window, trying to remove some washing, overbalanced and fell. Somehow she managed to grasp the line. Her screams were quickly picked up by passersby in the street below.

Shouting out to Lydia to keep her courage, Charles Davis crept out of one of the nearby windows and, asking his wife to hold his ankles with both hands, stretched out his left arm and caught hold of Lydia's dress and pulled the terrified tot towards him until his wife managed to catch her.

AGONIZING SCENE - FEARFUL POSITION OF A GIRL

93. *The brave rescue of Lydia Stevens in Newcastle. Somehow the youngster got herself hung out to dry!*

BOYS WILL BE GIRLS

Many a tale has been handed down about folk who've spent their whole lives passing themselves off as members of the opposite sex. Some were not discovered until after death, but others were found out by sheer accident.

The following story of an 18-year-old Dutch runaway is taken from the *Newcastle Journal* (21.11.1872). The tale is most tastefully recounted, though whether by design only the reporter knows:

…When the vessel was in Shields harbour a boy presented himself to the captain and owner, and expressed a desire to join the ship as an apprentice. This was taken into consideration, and as the boy possessed a good figure fully in keeping with the profession he was about to adopt, they decided to bind him for three years, which was executed on the usual terms and in legal form. The boy commenced his work on board, and continued to do his duty on the passage out, to the general satisfaction of all on board, passing through all the varied and hazardous duties of a sailor, going aloft, assisting in reefing and stowing sails etc. in bad weather, and after arrival in this port working at the cargo until two days ago, when his career was interrupted by the suspicions of his fellow sailors in the forecastle as to his sex. Their curiosity could be no longer bridled, and they satisfied themselves that there were good grounds of suspicion. One of the number was then deputed to inform the captain of his female apprentice, who was forthwith called into the cabin, and, not being able to produce articles to the contrary, she was obliged to confess and own her sex.

The story has a happy ending as the girl continued to sail the seas, signing articles as a stewardess.

HARD LINES

By the 1870s more and more children were *creeping like a snail, unwillingly to school*. For various reasons some parents wished their offspring to stay at home or help them at work.

School fees in Monkwearmouth in 1873 were 4d per week per child. If pupils had an atrocious attendance rate their parents were taken to court. One mother argued that she had to *see to the pigs* and needed her daughter to do the housework. Another protested that her son did not possess a pair of shoes. Whatever excuse was given, the reasons for non-attendance were usually financial. Mrs Farrant argued: *I have six children; my husband's average earnings are £1 per week and I find it very 'hard lines'.*

With the large number of children in Victorian families, the unfortunate eldest daughter often had her own childhood sacrificed by becoming mother's little helper, changing, feeding and caring for siblings just a few years younger than herself. 11-year-old Arthirina Cape had answered *Yes Miss* to the register just six times out of a possible 252. Her mother appeared in court arguing that the young girl needed no further education. Let's listen in to the proceedings:

MRS CAPE: *She is a very good scholar. She can take up the papers and read almost anything that is in them. I want her at home to nurse the child and to do house-work.*
MAYOR: (reading the letter that the mother had sent). *Don't you think that if you were to learn to spell yourself it would be a great advantage to you?*
MRS CAPE: *Yes, but when Mr Johnston [truant officer] came to my house he was so impudent he disturbed me. If he had not gone away when he did he would have got something.* (Laughter).
MAGISTRATE'S CLERK: *This is no credit to you.*
MRS CAPE: *I do not know whether it is a credit or not. I consider the school-board is just a money-making business.* (Laughter).
MAYOR: *We will have to teach you different.*
MRS CAPE: *You will have a job perhaps to teach me different, I can assure you.*
MAYOR: *You seem to be very impertinent*
MRS CAPE: *I do not think ____*
MAYOR: *You are not allowed to think on these questions. Other people think for you.*
MRS CAPE: *Oh, indeed: people's not allowed to think now, hah!*
MAYOR: *You are fined 5s. and you will be fined again if you do not send your child to school.*
MRS CAPE: *How can I pay when her 'da' has not worked these two months?*

Though not the town's best speller, Mrs Cape won begrudging respect from all in court that day.

TWICE IN ONE NIGHT!

Travelling at night could be a risky business. In 1869 a 17-year-old butcher and friend set out in a spring cart from Trimdon Colliery to Hartlepool. As they were leaving Hart, a dark figure, wielding a large bludgeon, suddenly emerged from the undergrowth and made a grab for the horse's head. The driver immediately coaxed the steed into a trot, leaving the would-be assailant stumbling in their wake. As they raced off an accomplice was spotted hiding behind a tree.

About a mile later, as the two were congratulating themselves over the evasive action, they were attacked a second time when a man darted out from behind a hedge and tried to board the cart from behind. There was no room for any fellow-travellers and the second assailant's hold was soon relinquished following a well-directed blow from the butcher's fist.

A DEAD LETTER

In 1874 Mr Shafto, a member of the Liberal Party, despatched a formal police order banning one Mr Anthony from voting in the forthcoming election. A few days later he received the following, surprising reply:

Shotton Colliery August 26th. 1874.
To Mr James Shafto,
I am very sorry to inform you that I have been dead eighteen months, and if you want to see me, you will find me in Shotton Colliery Churchyard.

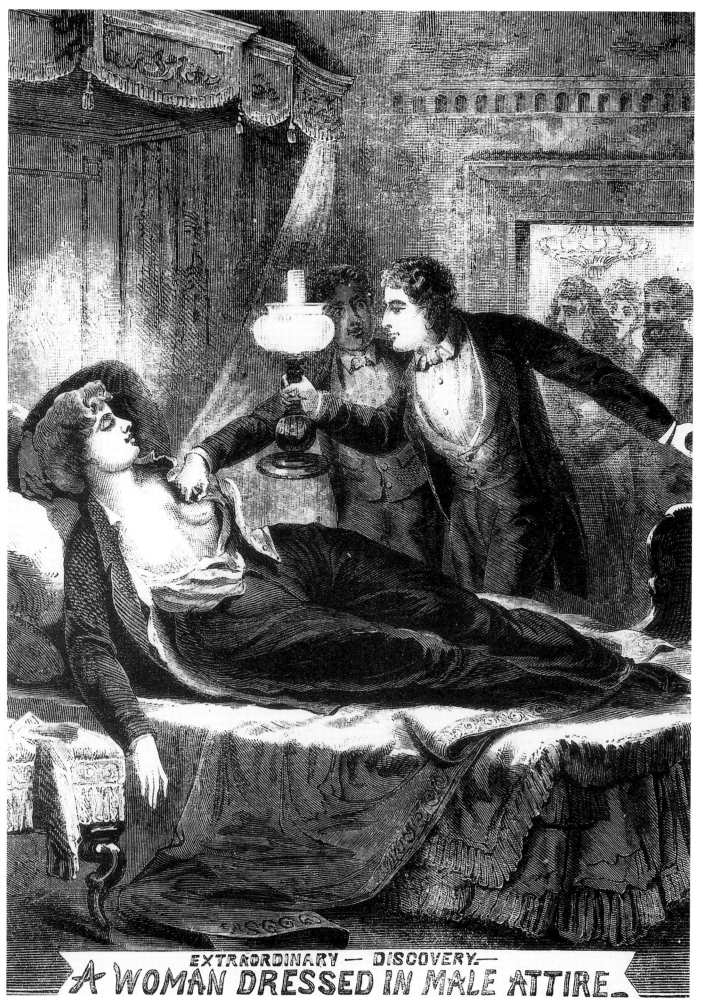

EXTRAORDINARY — DISCOVERY —
A WOMAN DRESSED IN MALE ATTIRE.

94. Newcastle, 1872. An 18-year-old Dutch female runaway, who had joined a ship in the guise of a male, was forced to confess her secret after not being able to produce articles to the contrary.

CURIOUS CATASTROPHE WHILST BATHING

95. A warning to ladies everywhere, from an 1870's girl: don't go swimming in the Tyne with your wig on!

LET HER RIP

Antagonism towards councils, their petty rules, bureaucrats and army of brain-dead jobs'worths, has been with us since local authorities were first formed. In 1913, Ralph White accepted that his two-roomed slum in Berwick would have to be demolished, but he flatly objected to being held financially responsible for clearing the site. There appeared to be a rule for everything and the individual rarely won. Ralph addressed the Council Demolition Board:

I see it's no use: it's all cut and dried. Let her rip. I want to know who is paying the piper for clearing the debris. I am not in a position to as I am out of work.

He was then informed by the mayor that the authority would do the job but take his site as compensation. Soon to be homeless and broke, Patrick could do no more than begrudgingly accept the situation:

If she has got to come down you will have to remove her yourself. Nothing from nothing leaves nothing; you cannot take the breeches off a naked man.

BREACH OF THE PEACE AT SPENNYMOOR

Most miners settled their differences in the bare-knuckle tradition. On rare occasions a policeman was summoned to physically restrain one macho party from beating the other to pulp. When P.C. Robinson arrived outside a Spennymoor property one bitter day in February in 1873, he was confronted by a man stripped to the waist. The semi-naked figure was holding his guard high in the fashion of a pugilist. Whilst skipping and shadow-boxing an imaginary opponent, the protagonist hurled insults at a miner from Page Bank colliery, who was hiding in the house. The taunter was arrested on a charge of breaching the peace, and a short time later stood before the bench. The chairman first questioned the complainant. Neither he, nor the defendant, are named in the report:

CHAIRMAN: *Has he ever done so before?*
COMPLAINANT: *Yes, Sir, many times.*
CHAIRMAN: *What for?*
COMPLAINANT: *He says I have got his wife* (laughter). *The woman had three children when I married her, and I must say that she seemed to me to be a very tidy and sensible sort of woman* (great laughter).

96. Spennymoor, scene of many a late night brawl. In 1873 two miners clashed over the affections of the same woman. As one stood in the street, stripped to the waist assuming the pose of the pugilist, his opponent shouted threats through the door swearing that if the boxer did not decamp he would come and 'knock his brains out'.

CHAIRMAN: *Well we don't want the history of your courtship.*

P.C. Robinson then told the court that the defendant had been stripped to the waist and was shouting at the top of his voice.

CHAIRMAN (to prisoner) *What have you to say to this? You know you had no right to go and put this man in bodily fear.*

DEFENDANT: *Well Sir, you see he has got my wife. She is married to him and she is married to me* (laughter). *I have had four children to this woman* (roars of laughter). *What I mean gentlemen is she has had four children to me and she ran away and left me* (renewed laughter). *This man wrote her letters enticing her away and she went.*

CHAIRMAN: *All that won't justify you in going to the man's house and threatening his life.*

DEFENDANT: *He threatened me first, Sir. He shouted through the door that if I did not go away he would come out and knock my brains out, and I invited him out to try* (great laughter).

COMPLAINANT: *That is quite untrue, Sir. He called the woman everything, and I have been married to her eight years and she is as decent a woman as ever stood in two shoes. I cannot believe that the likes of such a man as that is the father of the children the woman had when I married her. If he is I am ashamed to think they have any connection with him.*

The dispute seemed set to run and run as the defendant was bound over for three months to keep the peace.

GEORDIE FAWBERT OF DARLINGTON

There was no shortage of characters in Victorian times. Every town and village could boast a few eccentrics and lovable rogues who made their own rules and cared little for what people thought of them.

Darlington's much-loved oddball was Geordie Fawbert, a man of many professions. Geordie was born in 1874 and is still remembered by many as he lived to the ripe old age of 86. From his early days in Parkgate, Geordie was his own man. His house stood out from the others as its windows were tied together with string and blocked with packing cases. Stories circulated that he kept his horse in the front room. When Geordie told a pal that the stench in his bedroom was overpowering because of the beast stabled below, his friend enquired why he did not open the windows. *No way* was the reply. *The pigeons 'll get out.*

Geordie was the stereotype of the northern working-class man, the Andy Capp of Darlington. He rarely changed his clothes and was always to be found in a pair of baggy old trousers, a threadbare tweed jacket, muffler and flat cap. One year, having hobbled around for six months, Geordie undertook a rare visit to the doctor. Upon removing his sock with great difficulty, the cause of his pain, a shirt collar stud, was discovered. It had been missing for six months.

Not surprisingly, given his singular way of life, Geordie appeared before the beak on several occasions. He cared little for protocol and was once reprimanded for entering the witness box covered in soot. Geordie could not see the problem, this was the natural state for a chimney sweep.

97. Darlington's much loved eccentric Geordie Fawbert (centre) at his bicycle shop with his father and sister. Geordie was a wheeler-dealer who dabbled in all nature of jobs. One of his many scams when he worked as a fishmonger was to put his produce into coal sacks and 'refrigerate' them overnight in the River Skerne.

It was in the world of work that the similarity between himself and the fictional Andy Capp was at odds. Among Geordie's many other jobs were that of a cycle shop owner, coal merchant, fishmonger, mussel merchant, bus proprietor, caravan site owner and property speculator. Geordie was a grafter. Buying mussels from Whitby, Geordie would sell them at Darlington market. The fish he purchased at Hartlepool he would bring home on a No 24 United bus. With the Darlington market being held on a Monday, Geordie saved any unsold fish. These he would stuff into coal sacks and 'refrigerate' in the River Skerne for the Middlesbrough market two days later.

Eccentrics and oddballs are magnets for children and Geordie was no exception. Youngsters would gather round his stall and chant their home-made nursery-rhyme:

> Geordie Fawbert, he sells fish,
> For three ha'pence it'll make a tasty dish.
> But don't buy it, don't buy it,
> It smells when you fry it.

Geordie could turn his hand to anything that might make a bob or two. On many occasions he lost money but, undeterred, would soon bounce back and set up a new venture. He introduced the first Darlington to Middleton bus service and later ran his own coal business. No area of his Model T Ford was wasted as buckets of coal were transported under the seats. Then, like all astute men, Geordie saw there was money in property and promptly paid £1,000 in cash for seven houses in Four Riggs.

As Andy had his Flo, Geordie had his Maud, some twenty-five years his junior. Maud put many of Geordie's enterprising ideas into action. She would load fish at Bank Top Station and, with the help of a wooden cart, transport her goods to market. Once she had sold the fish, she would purchase empty wooden orange and onion crates, load them onto her fish-free cart and wheel them home. The crates would be chopped up, tied in bundles and sold for firewood.

Geordie was a man who changed with the times and always had an eye out for a quick shilling even if, at times, he bent the rules a little. He died in 1960. Had he lived a few more years there's no doubt as to which Frank Sinatra song his mourners would have requested at his funeral.

TOMMY ON THE BRIDGE AND FRIENDS

> Horatious kept the Tiber Bridge,
>   he fought in days of yore,
> Such a gallant feat of arms
>   ne'er was seen before,
> But another man, a bridge did keep,
>   above the Tyne, he stood,
> Blind at birth, he had to fight
>   hungering oft for food,
> With crippled arms and shabby clothes,
>   and most times weary legged,
> He shivered cold, in winter-time
>   yet he stayed and begged.

Newcastle and Gateshead were home to several characters including Captain Starkey, Cull Billy, Bugle-nosed Jack and Bold Archie. Probably the most eccentric, however, were the Gateshead three, Tommy on the Bridge, Sawdust Jack and Coffee John.

In 1842, Thomas Ferens was born blind and partially paralysed. He lost both his parents when he was only five. Unable to work, Tommy was forced to beg for a living. He eventually settled on a pitch on the Swing Bridge where he could be found every day between 11am and 4pm, except on Sundays. Shifting his weight from one leg to the other, he would stand in the middle of the bridge. In this way he ensured that he was technically neither in Newcastle nor Gateshead and could not therefore be arrested for begging by police from either town. As most pedestrians crossing the Swing Bridge did so in order to save the halfpenny toll on the High Level, his potential benefactors were for the most part strapped for cash themselves. He was often tormented by youngsters placing stones and buttons in his hands. These he would swiftly throw into the Tyne, rewarding the lads with a rich seam of swearwords. Worse than the boys were the factory lasses, said to be the bane of Tommy's life. They would deliberately taunt him until he volleyed forth a tirade of four letter expletives. As a local policeman remarked, his language was not *bad* it was *fertiliser*! Indeed it was deemed so offensive that questions concerning 'Tommy on the Bridge' were raised at council meetings. Not that Tommy was any great fan of petty officials, repeatedly threatening to sue them for compensation because of the number of times his 'trade' was interrupted by the bridge swinging. Let's listen to some of his reasoning:

'Aa'm gannin' to pitishun the Corporation to get the bridge alter'd; it dissint suit me, for whenivor ther's a ship cummin eethor up or' doon, aa hev to move off the Swing; aa waddint mind if they paid us for'd, but aa get no compensayshun, an aa think it's a blow'd shame ov ennyboddy tryin' t prevent a man myekin a livin.'

Tommy was often his own worst enemy. Said to earn between 4d and 1s per day, he would often contemptuously throw coppers (coins) into the river. On one occasion a kindhearted female pensioner pressed three pennies into his hand. It was not one of Tommy's better days:

Coppers! Ye're a canny body wi' yer saft soaping an' yer lousy threepence! Ah divant want em onyways!

With this he threw the three coins into the Tyne.

When times were really hard Tommy would fall back onto his boxer-publican friend Will Curley who would stand him a few bevvies and make sure he didn't starve. Tommy generally lodged with a widow in Gateshead but on at least one occasion was imprisoned for two weeks.

Normally the police would merely warn him about his language. One day a policeman from Gateshead and one from Newcastle were sent to Swing Bridge to deal with a minor fracas. Tommy, standing as always with one foot either side of the central line, argued that neither officer was 'entitled' to him.

What'll we do? asked the policeman from Gateshead. With classic deference to the Wisdom of Solomon the Newcastle bobby replied, *Ah divant knaaw. Unless ye take half to Gateshead and me half to Newcassel.*

In 1907, aged 65, Tommy collapsed in a snow storm on the Swing. He was helped to Bridge Street and was there found by police. Taken to Gateshead Workhouse Hospital, he died a short time later of *apoplexy accelerated by exposure to severe cold and weather.*

For decades Tommy had been a 'landmark'. Poems and songs were written about him, he was pointed out to visitors to the city and featured on postcards. Ironically, he was no more popular than at his funeral, which was attended by many of his tormentors and even reported in the local newspaper:

The funeral procession passed through double lines of spectators from his house in Canon Street to the Gateshead Cemetery. Around the house was a great throng, chiefly composed of women and children; and when the hearse arrived, a great crowd closed in. Two policemen had to keep the way clear for the underbearers.

The strange procession was led by about a dozen boys, one of whom carried a large wreath. This seems peculiar, as Tommy's pet aversion was the street boy who was wont to tease him. Throughout the entire course to the cemetery a large crowd assembled...This was the last of Tommy.

Sawdust Jack made his living from hawking (yes, you've guessed!) sawdust! He delivered the commodity to pubs in his wheelbarrow. Throughout his life, he kept himself fit and enjoyed being the centre of attention. He would race his pal 'Daft Martin' round the Butcher's Market every Saturday afternoon for a pound of sausages.

The pair also performed at Ginnett's Circus where they would fight for the 'Championship of the World'. With Martin blackened with burnt cork, and both contestants well greased, they set about each other in the ring for a supposed purse of £5. The winner never received more than eighteen pence.

Proud of his athletic prowess, Sawdust Jack told anyone and everyone who would listen that he intended to push a wheelbarrow full of sawdust from London to Newcastle. Over the next few days word spread that Jack had reached Peterborough or was on the outskirts of Doncaster. Finally sighted staggering through Team Colliery covered in mud, he was almost in a state of collapse. Hundreds of well-wishers turned out to line the route and greet the man who had completed such a feat of endurance. The truth, however, soon leaked out that Sawdust's journey had only commenced at Chester-le-Street.

The third member of the trio was Coffy Johnny who played the cornet, albeit not to everyone's taste. Playing outside the Black Horse on Kell's Lane, he was invited in by the locals to share a glass of ale. Johnny enthusiastically knocked back his pint, which, unbeknown to him, contained a large dose of 'jollup'. From that day on he gave the pub a wide berth.

98. And it's farewell from 'Sawdust', 'Coffee' and Tommy too.

Another occasion saw Johnny asked to play at a wedding. He was commissioned not by bride or groom but by a hot-headed Irishman who offered him several shillings to play 'Boyne Water' outside a certain house in Dunston.

As soon as the bridegroom heard the despised strain he dashed out and knocked the cornet out of the astonished player's hand. He then proceeded to kick the instrument about the street. From that day on Johnny had to make his living with a badly battered instrument.

Johnny's main claim to fame was that he had the same name as a character featured in the *Blaydon Races*. Whether he took his sobriquet from the song is unclear but he is certainly remembered by it:

The rain it poured aw the day,
an' made the groons quite muddy,
Coffy Johnny had a white hat on
they were shootin 'Whe stole the cuddy'

The real Coffee Johnny was a blacksmith from Winlaton, 6'6" in his socks, who acquired his nickname as a child. When other boys called at his house on the way to school he would always ask them to wait while he supped his coffee. The name stuck throughout his life.

The composer of the *Blaydon Races*, George Ridley, something of a character himself, certainly made the most of the 29 years of his very short life. Born in 1835 George was so badly injured by a runaway wagon at Crawshay's ironworks at the age of 20, that he had to find another means of making a living. As he convalesced he taught himself to versify, sing and mimic,

eventually joining the Tyneside Minstrels and quickly rising to the top of his profession. Though best remembered for the *Blaydon Races,* sung by Geordies all over the world, his other works vibrate with the sheer pleasure of being alive and young. Here are the opening lines from *Cushie Butterfield*::

I'm a broken hearted keelman
And I'm over head in luv,
With a young lass in Gateshead,
And I call her me duv,
Her name's Cushie Butterfield
and she sells yalla clay
And her cousin is a muckman
and they call him Tom Grey.

She's a big lass
she's a bonnie lass
an' she likes her beer
An' they call her Cushie Butterfield
an' aa wish she was here.

Though his melodies linger on, George Ridley, who contracted tuberculosis, departed this life in 1864. And we too must depart, leaving the old counties of Northumberland and County Durham.

I very much hope you've had a wicked read. If any mistakes have inadvertently been included, I would much appreciate hearing about them so they may be corrected if/when the book is reprinted.

STEVE JONES, NOTTINGHAM. September 1999.

ACKNOWLEDGEMENTS:

My main thanks must go to my brother Terry who spent five years in the North-East and has visited every pub in the good beer guide in the region. He knows the area very well and helped tremendously with the research, uncovering fascinating stories from pit village to large industrial city.

Librarians the length and breadth of the counties did an excellent job despite being weighed down with endless bureaucracy.

Viv Foster, my editor, is merciless with me and cuts and rewrites making the text a far smoother read than would otherwise be the case. I couldn't do without her but as I have access to the computer after she's finished I do restore some of my observations that are not exactly P.C. Please don't tell.

STEVE JONES, NOTTINGHAM, SEPTEMBER, 1999.

ILLUSTRATION ACKNOWLEDGEMENTS:
ILLUSTRATED POLICE NEWS: 3, 30, 32, 42, 42a, 43, 44, 49, 50, 54, 67, 69, 70, 71,73, 74, 76, 77, 80, 81, 87, 90, 93, 94, 95.
TYNE AND WEAR ARCHIVES SERVICE: 13, 14, 15, 16, 17, 18, 19, 20, 21, 23, 24, 25, 26, 38, 55, 56, 57, 58, 64, 65.
SOUTH TYNESIDE LIBRARIES:1, 2, 4, 5, 36, 92.
GEORGE COLLEY, MEMORY LANE PRINTS: 9,10, 22, 39, 51.
BERWICK-UPON-TWEED RECORD OFFICE : 46, 75.
BOWES MUSEUM, DURHAM COUNTY COUNCIL: 11, 12.
DARLINGTON LIBRARY: 47, 96, 97.
NEWCASTLE LIBRARIES AND INFORMATION SERVICE: 7, 60, 62, 78, 79, 88, 89.
WARD PHILIPSON GROUP LTD: 8, 27, 45, 52, 53.
GATESHEAD COUNCIL LIBRARIES AND ARTS: 6, 86, 98.
DURHAM RECORD OFFICE: 33
ARTS, LIBRARIES AND MUSEUMS DEPT., DURHAM COUNTY COUNCIL: 66
NORTHUMBERLAND RECORD OFFICE: 59.
ALL OTHER PICTURES FROM THE AUTHOR'S COLLECTION

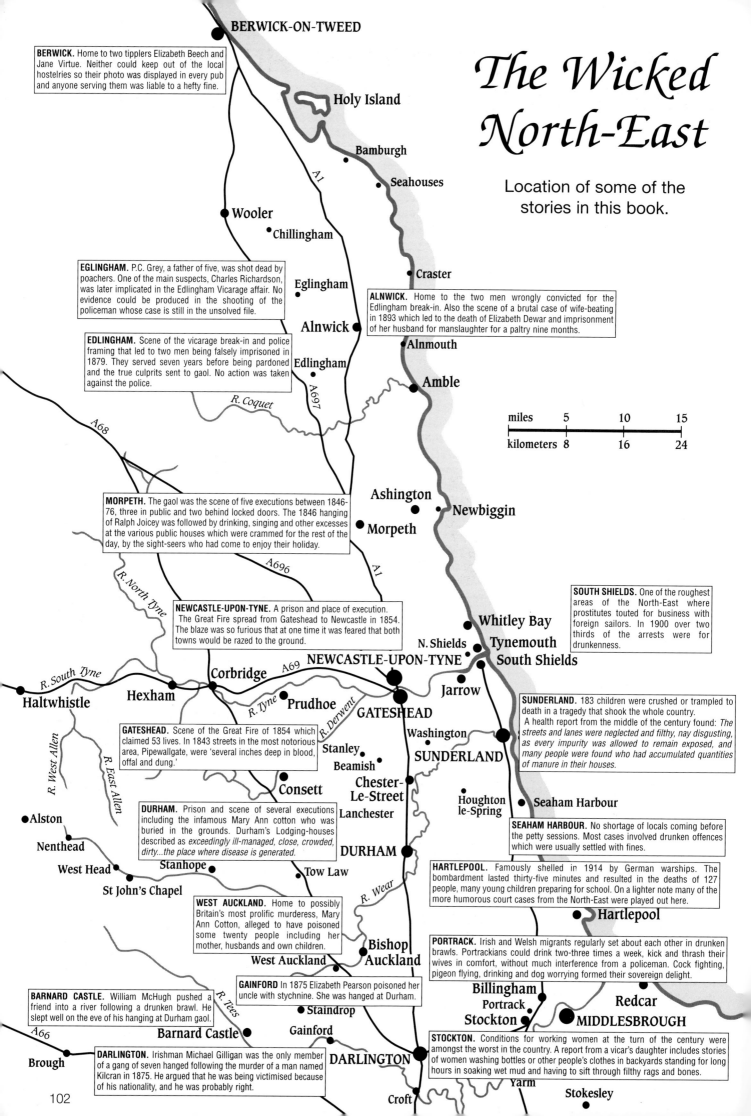

The Wicked North-East

Location of some of the stories in this book.

BERWICK-ON-TWEED

Holy Island

Bamburgh

Seahouses

BERWICK. Home to two tipplers Elizabeth Beech and Jane Virtue. Neither could keep out of the local hostelries so their photo was displayed in every pub and anyone serving them was liable to a hefty fine.

Wooler

Chillingham

Craster

EGLINGHAM. P.C. Grey, a father of five, was shot dead by poachers. One of the main suspects, Charles Richardson, was later implicated in the Edlingham Vicarage affair. No evidence could be produced in the shooting of the policeman whose case is still in the unsolved file.

Eglingham

Alnwick

ALNWICK. Home to the two men wrongly convicted for the Edlingham break-in. Also the scene of a brutal case of wife-beating in 1893 which led to the death of Elizabeth Dewar and imprisonment of her husband for manslaughter for a paltry nine months.

Alnmouth

EDLINGHAM. Scene of the vicarage break-in and police framing that led to two men being falsely imprisoned in 1879. They served seven years before being pardoned and the true culprits sent to gaol. No action was taken against the police.

Edlingham

Amble

R. Coquet

A697

A68

miles 5 10 15

kilometers 8 16 24

Ashington

Newbiggin

MORPETH. The gaol was the scene of five executions between 1846-76, three in public and two behind locked doors. The 1846 hanging of Ralph Joicey was followed by drinking, singing and other excesses at the various public houses which were crammed for the rest of the day, by the sight-seers who had come to enjoy their holiday.

Morpeth

R. North Tyne

A696

A1

SOUTH SHIELDS. One of the roughest areas of the North-East where prostitutes touted for business with foreign sailors. In 1900 over two thirds of the arrests were for drunkenness.

NEWCASTLE-UPON-TYNE. A prison and place of execution. The Great Fire spread from Gateshead to Newcastle in 1854. The blaze was so furious that at one time it was feared that both towns would be razed to the ground.

Whitley Bay

N. Shields

Tynemouth

South Shields

R. South Tyne

Corbridge

A69

NEWCASTLE-UPON-TYNE

Haltwhistle

Hexham

Prudhoe

R. Tyne

GATESHEAD

Jarrow

R. Derwent

GATESHEAD. Scene of the Great Fire of 1854 which claimed 53 lives. In 1843 streets in the most notorious area, Pipewallgate, were 'several inches deep in blood, offal and dung.'

Washington

SUNDERLAND. 183 children were crushed or trampled to death in a tragedy that shook the whole country.
A health report from the middle of the century found: *The streets and lanes were neglected and filthy, nay disgusting, as every impurity was allowed to remain exposed, and many people were found who had accumulated quantities of manure in their houses.*

Stanley

Beamish

SUNDERLAND

R. West Allen

R. East Allen

Consett

Chester-Le-Street

Lanchester

Houghton le-Spring

Seaham Harbour

DURHAM. Prison and scene of several executions including the infamous Mary Ann cotton who was buried in the grounds. Durham's Lodging-houses described as *exceedingly ill-managed, close, crowded, dirty...the place where disease is generated.*

Alston

Nenthead

West Head

Stanhope

Tow Law

DURHAM

SEAHAM HARBOUR. No shortage of locals coming before the petty sessions. Most cases involved drunken offences which were usually settled with fines.

HARTLEPOOL. Famously shelled in 1914 by German warships. The bombardment lasted thirty-five minutes and resulted in the deaths of 127 people, many young children preparing for school. On a lighter note many of the more humorous court cases from the North-East were played out here.

St John's Chapel

R. Wear

WEST AUCKLAND. Home to possibly Britain's most prolific murderess, Mary Ann Cotton, alleged to have poisoned some twenty people including her mother, husbands and own children.

West Auckland

Bishop Auckland

PORTRACK. Irish and Welsh migrants regularly set about each other in drunken brawls. Portrackians could drink two-three times a week, kick and thrash their wives in comfort, without much interference from a policeman. Cock fighting, pigeon flying, drinking and dog worrying formed their sovereign delight.

GAINFORD In 1875 Elizabeth Pearson poisoned her uncle with stychnine. She was hanged at Durham.

BARNARD CASTLE. William McHugh pushed a friend into a river following a drunken brawl. He slept well on the eve of his hanging at Durham gaol.

R. Tees

Staindrop

Billingham

Portrack

Redcar

Stockton

MIDDLESBROUGH

Gainford

Barnard Castle

A66

STOCKTON. Conditions for working women at the turn of the century were amongst the worst in the country. A report from a vicar's daughter includes stories of women washing bottles or other people's clothes in backyards standing for long hours in soaking wet mud and having to sift through filthy rags and bones.

Brough

DARLINGTON. Irishman Michael Gilligan was the only member of a gang of seven hanged following the murder of a man named Kilcran in 1875. He argued that he was being victimised because of his nationality, and he was probably right.

DARLINGTON

Yarm

Croft

Stokesley

CRIMINAL AND SOCIAL HISTORY THEY DIDN'T DARE TEACH YOU AT SCHOOL!

TITLE: **LONDON... THE SINISTER SIDE**
AUTHOR: **STEVE JONES**
ISBN: **1-87000-000-5**
SIZE: **A4**
PAGES: **88**
ILLUSTRATIONS/PHOTOS: **104**
PRICE: **£6.99**
NOTES: **AVAILABLE IN JAPANESE.**

Our first and best-selling book which has been in print since 1986 with reprints well into double figures. Topics covered range from early executions to the Kray Twins. 15 pages are devoted to the hunt for Jack the Ripper and the book illustrated with over 100 photographs and pictures.

TITLE: **WICKED LONDON**
AUTHOR: **STEVE JONES**
ISBN: **1-870000-01-3**
SIZE: **A4**
PAGES: **96**
ILLUSTRATIONS/PHOTOS: **96**
PRICE: **£6.99**
NOTES: **AVAILABLE IN JAPANESE.**

In two parts. The first half of the book examines the most notorious murder cases in the capital including Dr. Crippen, Christie, Haig – 'the acid-bath' murderer and many more. The second half is centred around social life – food, drink and leisure – and conflict within the capital, including chapters on the often violent struggle of the women's movement and tragic tales of the Blitz.

TITLE: **THROUGH THE KEYHOLE**
AUTHOR: **STEVE JONES**
ISBN: **1-870000-02-1**
SIZE: **A4**
PAGES: **104**
ILLUSTRATIONS/PHOTOS: **109**
PRICE: **£6.99**
NOTES: **AVAILABLE IN JAPANESE.**

A peek at private lives, from prince to pauper, in the eighteenth and nineteenth centuries. 'Through the Keyhole' reveals the secrets of what went on behind locked doors in workhouses, slums and palaces – with detailed court accounts of adultery and sexual scandal. In later chapters we look at how the masses spent their limited leisure time in pubs and penny playhouses.

TITLE: **CAPITAL PUNISHMENTS**
AUTHOR: **STEVE JONES**
ISBN: **1-870000-03-X**
SIZE: **A4**
PAGES: **104**
ILLUSTRATIONS/PHOTOS: **106**
PRICE: **£7.99**
NOTES: **AVAILABLE IN JAPANESE.**

A detailed look at a variety of cases coming before the 'beak' in Victorian times. Assault and wife-beating were only too common following serious sessions in the ale-houses. The book follows those convicted into the horrors of the Victorian prison system where silence was often the rule and the food 'scarce fit for hogs'. Many of the stories of the atrocious conditions are related by the prisoners themselves.

TITLE: **IN DARKEST LONDON**
AUTHOR: **STEVE JONES**
ISBN: **1-870000-04-8**
SIZE: **A4**
PAGES: **88**
ILLUSTRATIONS/PHOTOS: **79**
PRICE: **£6.99**

The book covers the period 1900-39 and relates first hand stories of prostitutes, criminals and backstreet abortionists. Details of the bombing raids in world war one are followed by tales of the General Strike of 1926 and an in depth look at Mosley's racist marches in the East End that resulted in serious violence and disruption. Light relief is provided with the extraordinary life of the prostitute's padre who ended his days in a lion's cage.

TITLE: **WHEN THE LIGHTS WENT DOWN**
AUTHOR: **STEVE JONES**
ISBN: **1-870000-05-6**
SIZE: **A4**
PAGES: **104**
ILLUSTRATIONS/PHOTOS: **91**
PRICE: **£7.99**

We've all heard the stories about the civilian population during WW2 pulling together, singing patriotic songs in crowded air-raid shelters and accepting the wartime privations in good heart. Indeed many did, but there was a sizeable minority who were determined to help themselves rather than their country. German bombers facilitated entry to other people's houses, and undercover of the blackout, looters set out on their gruesome treasure trove. Both crime figures and the prison population rose as offenders from black-marketeers to murderers sought to profit from the chaotic conditions.

TITLE: **NOTTINGHAM... THE SINISTER SIDE**
AUTHOR: **STEVE JONES**
ISBN: **1-870000-06-4**
SIZE: **A4**
PAGES: **104**
ILLUSTRATIONS/PHOTOS: **110**
PRICE: **£7.99**

Although internationally famous for being the home of Britain's most famous outlaw, Robin Hood, Nottingham, like all large cities, has housed tens of thousands of lawbreakers with no intention whatsoever of giving to the poor. The most infamous murders include 'Nurse Waddingham who poisoned two of her patients for their inheritance, and Herbert Mills, who executed 'the perfect murder' in order to sell his story to the newspapers – both were hanged.

TITLE: **LANCASHIRE LASSES... THEIR LIVES AND CRIMES**
AUTHOR: **STEVE JONES**
ISBN: **1-870000-07-2**
SIZE: **A4**
PAGES: **104**
ILLUSTRATIONS/PHOTOS: **107**
PRICE: **£7.99**

Life for Lancashire lasses in Victorian times often followed the path from mill or mine to marriage and maternity. On average they fell pregnant eight times and would raise their children as they themselves had been raised – in grinding poverty.

The temptation to escape the hardships was too great for many. Some would turn to crime, some to the bottle and some to both. Offenders were paraded in the dock on charges ranging from picking pockets to prostitution.

TITLE: **MANCHESTER... THE SINISTER SIDE**
AUTHOR: **STEVE JONES**
ISBN: **1-870000-09-9**
SIZE: **A4**
PAGES: **104**
ILLUSTRATIONS/PHOTOS: **103**
PRICE: **£7.99**

With the presence of over 100 photographs and illustrations, join us in a trip back in time to meet the incorrigible rogues, vagabonds and thieves in Victorian Manchester and the atrocious conditions endured by the vast majority of the population.

TITLE: **BIRMINGHAM... THE SINISTER SIDE**
AUTHOR: **STEVE JONES**
ISBN: **1-870000-14-5**
SIZE: **A4**
PAGES: **104**
ILLUSTRATIONS/PHOTOS: **133**
PRICE: **£7.99**

NOTES: **THIS BOOK IS EXTREMELY POPULAR, THE FIRST PRINT SELLING OUT IN ELEVEN WEEKS. HAS BEEN FEATURED ON SEVERAL RADIO AND TELEVISION PROGRAMMES.**

'Pickpockets, petty thieves, prostitutes, drunks, murderers and wife-beaters galore people its pages staring back at the reader from police 'mug-shots' with grim resignation, pathos or rebellion in their eyes sandwiched between spine-chilling 'penny-dreadful' illustrations portraying scenes of red murder of callous brutality, each of which for a fleeting moment in time, shocked the un-shockable!' (Black Country Bugle).

WICKED PUBLICATIONS

Lavishly illustrated and studiously researched, our original stories and photographs would certainly interest students (GCSE to degree level), local historians, social historians, genealogists and criminologists – but above all they are aimed at the general reader.

To date our satisfied customers total over 250,000.

SPECIAL OFFER TO INDIVIDUAL CUSTOMERS
ORDER FIVE DIFFERENT BOOKS – GET THE SIXTH ONE FREE. ORDER EIGHT DIFFERENT BOOKS – GET TWO EXTRA FREE. JUST FILL IN THE COUPON WITH SIX/TEN TICKS AND PAY FOR FIVE/EIGHT.

TERMS AND CONDITIONS

INDIVIDUAL SALES

We supply orders to the general public at the prices listed below. Wicked Publications pay all postage and packing within the U.K. and books will be sent within twenty-four hours of an order being received. Cheques should be made payable to **Wicked Publications**. At the moment we cannot accept credit cards. If you would like the books signed or dedicated please mention this with the order.

BUSINESS

We have accounts with all major booksellers and museum/visitor shops. Our general terms are 35% sale or return, if they don't sell we will take the book back if in resalable condition. We can confidently make this promise as returns over ten years have been minimal. We may give better terms for large orders or swift payment or to regular customers, everything is negotiable, please phone.

ORDER FORM

PLEASE SEND ORDER ALONG WITH CHEQUE TO **WICKED PUBLICATIONS AT 222, HIGHBURY ROAD, BULWELL, NOTTINGHAM NG6 9FE, ENGLAND. TEL: 0115 975 6828.**

TITLE	PRICE	NO OF COPIES
LONDON... THE SINISTER SIDE	£6.99	
WICKED LONDON	£6.99	
THROUGH THE KEYHOLE	£6.99	
CAPITAL PUNISHMENTS	£7.99	
IN DARKEST LONDON	£6.99	
WHEN THE LIGHTS WENT DOWN	£7.99	
NOTTINGHAM... THE SINISTER SIDE	£7.99	
LANCASHIRE LASSES... THEIR LIVES AND CRIMES	£7.99	
MANCHESTER... THE SINISTER SIDE	£7.99	
BIRMINGHAM... THE SINISTER SIDE	£7.99	
NORTHUMBERLAND AND DURHAM... THE SINISTER SIDE	£7.99	
*Postage (where applicable)	£	*(ALL POSTAGE IS FREE WITHIN THE U.K. ADD £1.50 PER BOOK MAINLAND EUROPE AND £3 U.S.A., CANADA, AUSTRALIA AND NEW ZEALAND).
TOTAL	£	

Name...

Address..

....

....

....Post Code.................................